A HANDBOOK OF
SCOTLAND'S
TREES

A HANDBOOK OF
SCOTLAND'S
TREES

or, The Tree Planter's Guide
to the Galaxy

Revised edition

REFORESTING SCOTLAND

edited by Fi Martynoga

Saraband

Published by Saraband
3 Clairmont Gardens
Glasgow, G3 7LW
www.saraband.net

Reforesting Scotland is a membership organisation
dedicated to supporting and promoting woodland
restoration, along with a healthy and prosperous
forest culture. To find out more about current
projects or join Reforesting Scotland, see
www.reforestingscotland.org.

Reforesting Scotland acknowledges subsidy from Forestry Commission
Scotland towards the initial publication of this volume.

ISBN: 9781908643827

Printed and bound in Great Britain by Clays Ltd, Elcograf S.p.A.

3   5   7   9   10   8   6   4

Cover and page 2: *'Holme Fen Birches' (print © Carry Akroyd).*

CONTENTS

PREFACE

This book is aimed as much at the beginner as it is at those already engaged in planting trees. Anyone who wants to know more about tree species, and would like a Scottish guide with some history and lore, should find it useful.

Beginners with only some garden trees to plant, or perhaps a small area of land, should gain lots of basic information and many useful tips in 'How to Plant a Tree' and 'What Tree to Plant'. Those who are ready for more ambitious planting should read on. The sections on collecting, storing and sowing seed are drawn from practical experience. The one on the legal framework for native seed collection offers a succinct reference guide to a complex subject, and those on planting larger areas and on no-fence planting have a wealth of useful information on how to get trees into different (and often difficult) planting sites.

Much of the material gathered here was first published as articles in the Reforesting Scotland Journal, (originally *The Tree Planter's Guide to the Galaxy*) where they found an enthusiastic audience over a number of years. For a long time before the original 2011 edition was compiled we had intended to revise and republish them, to capture the breadth of expertise and useful information they contain. Each piece was written by a different author, all (bar one) of whom have been contacted, though some who were retired when they wrote their pieces are now very old. They have all been generous enough to devote time to updating and improving what they originally set down. Their styles vary greatly. We are privileged to have absolutely state-of-the-science accounts from leading experts such as Professor Donald Pigott on lime trees and Dr A.L. Primavesi on wild roses, as well as Professor Stephen Woodward and his research associate Stuart Fraser, who have provided the new material for this updated edition on invasive pests and pathogens. These expert contributions are complemented by much more earthy accounts from practical, hands-on tree planters, too many to name. They are united by their enthusiasm for 'their' species. Such passionate interest makes any writing more vivid.

You will not find identical subsection headings for all the species in Part 2, the tree profiles section of the book, as each species dictates its own needs. Natives like oak, ash and hazel have their local lore, for instance; exotic species like lodgepole pine, Douglas fir and larch do not. The section on willow is twice as long as most because it includes detailed notes on how to establish your own willow bed for practical cropping. Let's hope more people are moved to do so as the oil age wanes and baskets make a comeback.

The list of tree species may seem eccentric, but it represents pretty well all those you are likely to meet growing in Scotland, not just the natives. If the monkey puzzle seems a particularly odd one to include, read its story, which has unexpected links to Scottish botanists in both the past and the present. And please don't assume that we have completely failed to cover all the exotic conifers you might meet in a plantation. They may not have their own profile, but most are mentioned with trees from the same location in the world, especially in the section on Douglas fir.

You will find that climate change receives several references but is not dealt with in depth. The main reason for this is that the majority of our native trees, and a good number of those we have introduced to the British Isles, have a very wide natural range. This means that we can continue to plant most of them with confidence, as they are likely to be able to withstand a good deal of change in climatic conditions.

That is good news, for in a world where we have so little control over the processes that bring about such things as climate change and invasive pests and diseases, planting trees is one of the really constructive things we can do. It may not solve the problems but it can bring you pleasure, satisfaction, hope, beauty, good fellowship, and can be constructive in a thousand ways. Involve children in the process of planting and you may be awakening a delight in the natural world that, like the trees they plant, could remain with them for a lifetime. So, if you haven't planted any trees yet, or if you want to plant many more, here is your guide!

Fi Martynoga

PART ONE

TREE CRAFT:
WHAT, WHERE,
WHY & HOW

SEEDS OF CHANGE

The expression 'planting seeds' has, both metaphorically and literally, a whiff of subversion about it: the phrase suggests the quiet but powerful beginnings of change. As a literal deed, planting seeds and seedlings has sometimes been an act of affirmation; in different ages and in different places it carries slight differences of meaning. You might be planting grasses in the face of encroaching desert, citrus orchards in the face of starvation, or a humble window box in the face of the hegemony of the supermarket chains. It can be a strike back, an act of defiance in the face of a world gone wrong.

Tree planting had these politically charged ingredients from its grassroots beginnings in the early 1980s in Scotland. Not that the likes of pioneers Ron Greer (Loch Garry Tree Group), Alan Drever (Scottish Native Woods Campaign) and Eoin Cox (Woodschool) were the first to plant trees for reasons other than the commercial, since the woodland establishment programme on Rhum had been going since 1957. But maybe they were the first to expressly link the act of tree planting with ambitious socio-political aims. At that particular time there was a sense of outrage, not just at the loss of the natural woodland vegetation throughout most of the land, but the way this had come about and was perpetuated by the wealthy few, largely for sport. The oft-quoted statistic of the time was that only 1 per cent of the land area of Scotland remained as native forest. The act of restoration of woodland and forest to the land appeared to be the perfect instrument of both ecological and political change, one that would bring about both a more equitable economy and a more sustainable land-use system in one fell swoop. The ambition was huge.

This vision has been more or less persistent throughout thirty years of what we may justifiably call 'the reforestation movement' in Scotland, a movement that is coming of age apace in the new century as community groups big and small, along with NGOs and some enlightened privately owned estates, reforest significant areas of open land in uplands and lowlands alike.

One of the first acts of several of the larger community 'buy-outs' has been to devise major woodland restoration plans. The three community land owners in Assynt, owning between them 27,000 hectares, whilst conserving and protecting vast tracts of existing but threatened birch wood, have planted and manage 1600 hectares of new native woodland. One of them, the Assynt Foundation, is conducting a feasibility study, looking to plant new native woodland in an area of up 5000 hectares in the coming years. Borders Forest Trust has planted 1750 hectares and has much larger areas in ecological management. Trees for Life is another of these visionary schemes (many of which were assisted by the Millennium Forest for Scotland), which have begun to change whole landscapes in ways only dreamed of in the '80s. And one gets the feeling that this is only the beginning.

The Scottish Government itself, through the Forestry Commission's forward strategy, has set a target of creating 143,000 sq km of new woodland in the next 40 years – an area the size of Aberdeenshire. Most of this will not be woodland for what one might call ecological restoration or social change, but nonetheless it will represent a change in the emphasis of land use towards a cellulose-based economy. The case for Scottish reforestation seemed compelling enough to the pioneers of the '80s, and the climate-change agenda has only served to strengthen that argument. In a world where 13 million hectares of forest are lost each year (including 6 million hectares of primary forests), our strike back against global environmental degradation may seem small, but it's something that we *can* do. Even if it won't stop global warming in itself, it might just help us survive in a world of fuel scarcity. And, by returning fertility and fecundity to large areas of degraded and infertile habitat, it may offer new ways of managing land to feed and shelter us in the future.

The reforestation movement has always concerned itself with the richness and diversity of economy that forest-based land-use systems can provide. Even the earliest editions of the *Tree Planter's Guide to the Galaxy*, from which the contents of this book are reborn, covered everything you could imagine from furniture making to wine making, from house building to horse logging. The journal (and the charity Reforesting Scotland, which produces it) continues to act as a mouthpiece for a constantly developing woodland economy. It plays a key role in inspiring and informing those involved in shaping the new woodland and woodland-based communities and businesses that thirty years of reforestation, followed by the next thirty, will allow to grow into shape.

The strength of the reforestation movement as a whole comes from its many parts. There has always been a happy symbiosis of the different organisations and groups that make up the whole. The journal of RS continues to bring together all aspects of the movement and is a the main visible strand of the charity's wider work. RS played a major part in the 2003 inception of the Community Woodland Association, which today represents more than 130 community woodland groups, of which the Loch Garry Tree Group from 1986, and Wooplaw Community Woodland from 1987, were probably the first.

The *modus operandi* of the organisation for many years has been to nurture an idea, to support the supporters of it, and spawn a new organisation that can grow into an independent body. Woods for All, funded by the Millennium Forest for Scotland, started work on access to woodland for disadvantaged people and has evolved into the Blarbuie Woodland project. The Scottish Wild Harvest Association is another flagship of this approach.

But there is still great work ahead on a number of fronts. In the last thirty years, state (and some private) forestry has come a long way towards integrating commercial forest management with landscape, recreation, watershed management, and wildlife conservation. But it is important to recognise that 48 per cent of the Scottish forest resource is of one species, the Sitka spruce, and that the prevailing model of commercial forestry is based on clearfell, mechanical ground preparation, artificial fertilisation, deer fencing and planting. This model can be easily enough criticised on the grounds of ecological damage – decreasing fertility over several rotations, erosion in some soils, disruptions of wildlife habitats, etc – but can be increasingly challenged in terms of fossil fuel reliance and declining soil carbon stocks. Its lack of diversity of species may pose a threat to its own sustainability in view of increasing and changing tree diseases and growth responses in response to climatic change.

But there are limits to how far one can 'tweak' the current prevailing forestry model without debilitating its commercial viability. Thus it may be more productive, and certainly more uplifting, to concentrate critical thinking on the fundamentally 'alternative' model that community-led forestry can offer for the future. Starting from a much wider set of premises and objectives, economic, social and spiritual, it is possible to envisage a model of forestry equipped for a different future. Indeed, perhaps one could see this as being designed for a different community of people with different priorities than those of today.

This is not to suggest that the current prevailing model of commercial forestry will be replaced in any short-term scenario. Plantation forests will be required to feed the pulp and particle mills, the construction sector and the power generating furnaces of the foreseeable future. But it *is* to suggest development of a complementary model with serious commitment and governmental support, a model that will be most naturally developed from the new community woodlands and largely native and broadleaved forests of various charities and progressive estates.

This model will be specifically designed for a range of future economic and ecological scenarios that we can already sketch out. These inevitably include either cripplingly high costs, or total unavailability, of fossil fuels; an increasing need for more self-reliance in food; and the need for more self-reliance in other natural resources, whether driven by actual shortages or a wish for independence from unpredictable global markets, from unpredictable climate change, from corporate facelessness, and the exploitation of remote people and land.

Key elements of this alternative model are likely to include: a diversity and significant quantity of broadleaved species to yield the hardwoods required for durable construction elements, including cladding and flooring; furniture and other artefact manufacture; extensive fuel wood production linked to local heat and power stations, district heating systems and individual appliances in rural locations close to supplies; agro-forestry systems where grazing and woodland are intentionally integrated to increase or diversify production; agro-forestry systems to produce tree food crops as well as cellulose; longer rotation cycles to produce large section timber for construction and as a means to minimise soil and habitat damage; wildwood for wildlife conservation and spiritual enjoyment; strict control of wild herbivores to maximise food production whilst minimising forest damage and fencing costs; natural regeneration or continuous cover management to reduce fossil fuel and other resource use, whilst increasing soil carbon reserves and minimising wildlife habitat damage; and integrated low-impact forest habitation, using local construction timber and wood energy.

There are plenty of existing models for all these things even within Europe. We have only to look at the broadleaved woodlands of France to see continuous-cover forestry producing highly economic hardwood timber in harmony with the production of non-timber forest crops such as nuts, venison and boar. We can look at Austria and Switzerland for close integration of a wealth of small and medium-sized timber manufacturing businesses working in symbiosis with foresters downstream and designers and architects upstream. In Norway we might look at pastoral grazing regimes within and around a variety of woodland types, again allowing a wide range of rural enterprises to flourish in an ecologically balanced patchwork.

We can look almost anywhere for better models than Scotland of how wild deer (and domestic grazing animals) can be integrated into a diversity of agricultural, woodland and wild harvest management systems. Indeed, until we face up to the scale of our archaic and wasteful approach to deer management, the potential benefits of a wide variety of existing and putative land uses will be denied to, or hampered within, a developing 'sustainable' Scottish land-use economy.

The ambitiousness of the Scottish reforestation project has an inspirational quality reaching out beyond itself and has featured in English, American and French media and scientific coverage. The Trees for Life project has attracted followers on an international scale to help put hundreds of thousands of trees in the ground. Whilst the act of restoring a significant area of Caledonian pine forest to the glens of Inverness-shire inspires folk to travel from around the world to give their help, the vision can also operate at even the smallest scale.

Planting a single fruit tree in your own garden may prove the starting point for bigger things. It is a simple act that almost anyone can perform. There is a very special pleasure in watching trees you have planted yourself grow tall. Get young children to plant trees and it may well prove a significant part of developing their environmental consciousness. Anyone who does it is given a sense of being able to change his or her immediate environment for the better. That may be a bleak and polluted urban environment or a deforested rural one, but either way, planting a seedling or a sapling tree may prove to be one of the most prescient acts we can make in our own lifetimes, and at this point in our planetary history.

Existing happily cheek by jowl with the land-use agenda and the political subtext, a part of the *Tree Planter's Guide to the Galaxy* was from the outset – just as the title implied – to disseminate practical information for tree planters, no matter at what scale or where on the planet they were doing it. A remarkable thing to remember is that knowledge of how to grow and establish the Scottish native tree and shrub species in the 1970s and '80s was invested in a tiny group of individuals. Foremost of these were Peter Wormell and Martin Ball, whose paper on nursery practice for the Scottish species, published in 1975 in *Scottish Forestry*, remains a classic. A part of this was reproduced in the very first issue of *TPGG*. Arguably, the knowledge was also secure in the hands of a very small number of Forestry Commission nurseries (now disappeared), but the special role of *TPGG* was to get that knowledge out into the hands of a whole new generation of enthusiastic planters.

A host of 'fish box' nurseries sprang up around Scotland in the '80s, and the arcane lore of seed collecting and stratification was popularised and secured once more. The tree nursery I ran with my then wife, Emma, in the '80s and '90s in west Sutherland, modelled closely on Peter Wormell's methods, hosted dozens of volunteers over a period of 15 years, many of whom went on to grow and plant trees. In those years we learned of tiny new nurseries as far afield as Orkney and the Western Isles. There was a new feeling that woodland belonged and could be re-established even in the most windswept of places. There was perhaps something especially encouraging in the fact that the *TPGG* was originally edited in a croft house on the north-west coast of Sutherland, as opposed to in a sheltered lowland glen.

More than twenty years later, the journal has a critical role at the heart of a movement that continues to develop new ideas and offshoots year on year. For practical advice on all aspects of woodland, or just sheer optimism, it's a read that is hard to beat. Through its pages you can feel the strength and scope of a genuinely grassroots and community-led movement inspired by the need for change. You will almost certainly also get a sense of how trees and new woodlands will continue to play a major role in changing the landscapes of Scotland this century, both ecological and political.

Bernard Planterose
Leckmelm Wood

Bernard and Emma Planterose started the TPGG in 1989 with Martin Howard while running a tree nursery and tree planting business in north-west Scotland. With Donald McPhillimy, they founded the charity RS in 1991, with the help of grant aid from the then HIDB and NCC. Andy Wightman was appointed the first RS Development Officer in 1992. Bernard now runs a design and build business near Ullapool using home-grown timber, some of it from his own woods.

HOW TO PLANT A TREE

First, using the observations in 'What Tree to Plant' and/or 'Planting Larger Areas', choose a suitable site and an appropriate tree for that site.

If you have grown your own seedlings, they will be either bare-rooted or container grown, probably in old pots. If you are buying from a nursery, you will either get bare-rooted or cell-grown trees. The latter are small seedlings grown in deep but narrow 'root-trainers' and usually sold in their second year.

Cell-grown trees are easy to plant. The root-trainers open so that the seedlings can be removed without pulling.

1 If you are planting into a grassy sward, you need to reduce the competition from the grass by 'screefing'. This means hacking back the turf from the immediate planting area. It is best done with a mattock, but you can use a spade, slashing horizontally under the turf to cut the roots of the grass and remove a sod of approximately 30cm square.

2 With a spade or a planting spear (which is like a miniature spade with a reinforced blade measuring about 10 x 20cm and particularly useful on rocky ground or scree), make a

hole in the centre of your cleared patch, taking care to go only as deep as the seedling requires. In good earth a mere slit, or two slits at 90° to each other in the shape of a cross, will suffice. You should ensure that the seedling is planted to the same depth as it was growing in the root-trainer, whilst being certain that the plug of roots is actually fully covered, to prevent it drying out.

3 If your protection is a vole guard (a small-diameter low tube), push a cane to support the tube into the planting slit first, then slip the seedling into the hole and trample it in with care. Next feed the guard gently over the seedling and cane, making sure the latter is stout and embedded enough to hold the guard firmly in place. If you are using a full-length tree tube, this will demand a much larger stake. It is best to bang this into the ground before you make the hole for the tree, to avoid damaging any roots.

Bare-rooted and container grown trees need larger holes.

1 Plant bare-rooted trees as soon as possible after lifting them. This is easy if you have grown your own. If you receive nursery stock, make sure that the tree roots remain covered, moist, and protected from frost.

2 Tackle potential competition from grass or weeds by 'screefing' (see above), using a mulch mat, or using cardboard with a mulch on top. The latter method is particularly good for fruit trees. A further way is to prepare each individual tree-planting site in advance by using a weed-killer such as glyphosate. This method is often necessary for large planting schemes, because it may be the only practicable way to ensure tree establishment, but is probably best avoided if you are only planting a few trees.

3 Dig a hole wide enough to take the spread-out roots of your seedling without cramping them, and deep enough to position the soil line (you will see this on the base of its stem)

exactly at ground level in the seedling's new site. In good ground an H-notch may suffice. This is made with three spade cuts in the shape of an 'H', so that you can undercut and roll back the ground away from the central cut to form the planting site. Take care not to cramp the roots.

4 Mound the earth slightly in the middle of your hole, so that the stem will sit on a slight rise, and the roots spread around it. Avoid scraping the earth, especially on clay soils, as this can cause 'glazing' and prevent good drainage.

5 If you are using a container-grown tree, remove the pot and gently tease the bottom of the root-ball, opening it so that the roots can start to spread out. This is important for trees that have stayed too long in a container and become pot-bound.

6 Position the seedling so that it sits comfortably in the hole. Back fill gently, treading the earth into the hole, and taking care that the seedling does not get buried too deeply. The root-ball of the container-grown tree should, however, be fully covered, as any roots left exposed will wick moisture away from the plant in dry weather.

7 Water the new tree and, ideally, do so again routinely in dry weather conditions throughout its first growing season. Mulching with lawn mowings, chipped bark, or other degradable material is a good way to preserve moisture and stop weed growth at the same time. Be careful not to pile the mulch against the stem of the tree, as it can damage it. A layer of cardboard under the mulch makes the mulch more effective.

Fi Martynoga

WHAT TREES TO PLANT

If you want to plant a few trees, you must have some land in mind for where you want to plant them. This chapter will help you to make some basic choices about the right species to choose for different environments. A few trees can be bought from a garden centre (any more than a few will break the bank). A larger number should be obtained from a specialist nursery (see www.treenurseryscotland.org), though they won't want to sell you less than a dozen at a time. It's not a good idea to order them online from a white delivery van, as you cannot guarantee their transit conditions. If you want to be involved with the whole process, there is plenty of advice in the subsequent chapters of this book about starting from scratch, collecting seed, and making a tree nursery of your own. Tree species shown in bold are all profiled in this book.

In gardens

Consider why you want to plant. Is it for privacy, visual enjoyment, to add habitat for wildlife, or a combination of these things? How big is your space? Can you combine fruit growing with one of these ends?

Hedges

If you want a hedge for privacy, don't rush to the garden centre and buy Leylandii. It grows more than a metre per year and does not give very much to our Scottish wildlife, apart from a few nesting sites. Consider **holly**, which is wonderfully thick and relatively quick-growing, has berries for decoration and for bird food, but has the downside of prickly clippings. **Yew** is slower-growing but will, in a few years, make a dense and easy-to-control hedge that only needs a single clip each year. Its berries feed thrushes and blackbirds, but children must be warned about yews. Every part of the tree except the red flesh of the berry is poisonous. **Beech** and hornbeam both make excellent hedges. In these situations they keep their brown leaves all winter, only shedding them at bud-burst in May, so they provide a good screen. If you live in the country, consider mixing **hawthorn** with **beech** for a thick, bird-friendly hedge, and even adding other species that are native to your area: **field maple, hazel, elder, blackthorn** and **holly** are the most likely ones.

Fruit trees and Forest gardening

If you have room for just one or two small trees, do think first about whether you could have productive, fruit-producing ones. Apples, pears, cherries and plums come on varying rootstocks that will give you trees of very specific shapes and sizes. Consult a specialist gardening book about this, and be content to buy from a garden centre, or from a specialist fruit nursery. Explain where you live and how high you are above sea-level, and you should get advice about what varieties might be suitable. The best-known Scottish apple, James Grieve, though delicious, is liable to canker and difficult to grow well. There are plenty of robust and climate-hardy eaters, like Ribston's pippin, Discovery, Sunset, Rosemary russet and Court pendu plat, and there are many varieties of cooking apples, from Bramleys to Grenadier, that will thrive in a wide range of Scottish gardens.

A productive and economical approach to growing fruit is that of Forest Gardening. You will need to look this up on the Internet or consult a book about it. The technique makes use of the multiple layers of natural woodland, from forest canopy to forest floor, and encourages you to use as many of these different niches as you can. Thus, you might grow large apples (or **crab apples**) as the canopy trees, **hazel** for nuts as a shrub layer, **brambles** and raspberries as the next layer down, and finally, perhaps strawberries on the fringes of your miniature forest. Somewhere in this carefully constructed wilderness, you might include **sea buckthorn** and **elder** for their luscious and vitamin-laden fruits. And don't forget the humble **dog rose**. Its flowers are one of the first delights of summer and its fruit, the hips, another fine source of Vitamin C.

Small trees to add height, colour and habitat

Our native trees, and some borrowed from south of the Border, offer plenty of colour and interest for a garden. Over the cycle of the seasons **rowan, wild cherry, bird cherry** (very pretty!), **hawthorn** and **whitebeam** all give blossom, then fruit for birds and squirrels, followed by autumn colour and interesting winter outlines. **Birches** are tall but don't occupy a big space; **hazels** are not as tall but will grow into substantial bushes, so can only be planted if you have plenty of room. **Field maple**, with their unusual bark and attractively shaped small leaves, are pretty all the year round, and provide good foraging for birds, without the disadvantage of shedding too much fertile seed. For this latter reason, **ash** and **sycamore** are difficult denizens of a small garden: their seedlings will take root anywhere.

Large trees for big gardens

If you are patient, plant an **oak** tree for future generations. If you want faster results, **limes** (though they are not quite native to Scotland) will grow into sizeable saplings within eight or nine years and substantial trees in twenty. Avoid driveways for limes, however, as the aphids that feed on them drop honey dew that makes a sticky mess on cars. If you have a craggy site with the right soil, consider some **Scots pine** and **birch**, and possibly **aspen**, the native poplar whose leaves will wave gently at you all summer long. Damp sites offer opportunities for **alder** and **willows**. You will have to look carefully at the section on willow to make the right choices from many possible species. Norway maples are very at home in Scottish gardens, and their autumn colour is hard to beat. **Elm** is probably not a good choice until the current round of Dutch elm disease subsides further, as this fungus routinely kills the trees off when they reach about 4m in height. If you have plenty of space, do encourage **ash** trees. They are miraculous plants, growing rapidly despite coming into leaf late and shedding their leaves early. They steal little light, provide good firewood, and will ultimately make fine mature trees. However, do beware of their propensity to seed themselves.

In neglected corners

If you live in the country and can identify places that need scattered trees, read the **No-fence planting** chapter. If you have spotted a site that might take a group of trees, and can engage a farmer or landowner with the idea, make a bid to fence it off. Any unwanted corner might have this potential. Rolls of old sheep netting and still-serviceable fencing posts are not usually hard to come by, so this need not cost you anything except time, effort and diplomacy. For any planting like this, study the remnants of native woodland around you and choose species that appear within them, using local provenance seed or local 'rescue' seedlings (ones that would otherwise be grazed off) wherever you can.

In an urban area, be on the lookout for odd bits of post-industrial land that could be enhanced by trees. Some people attempt this by guerrilla methods, simply planting where they can, without reference to owners. Others might prefer to get agreement, perhaps by showing all the ways in which trees could enhance the borders or corners of a site, no matter what the long-term plans for it may be. Your choice of species in this situation will be broad. It is still important to look at what flourishes in the landscape beyond the town or city, as you need to bring a sense of place back to tarmac and concrete. Use the locals. By this I mean not only local tree species but local people. If children and young people can be involved in the process of planting, the young trees are less likely to be vandalised. Make contact with existing community woodland groups in your area, or, depending on where you live, with trusts like Scottish Native Woods or Borders Forest Trust. They have staff and expertise and will respond to interesting suggestions, especially if you can form a small group of volunteers for ongoing management of new micro-woodlands in your area.

In school grounds

Urban schools may only have tarmac around them, which will severely limit what trees can be grown near them, possibly right down to things small enough to go in tubs. Small natives like the charming wee **dwarf birch** (*Betula nana*) or possibly **bird cherry** might supply this need. Alternatively, fruit trees on the smallest rootstocks can be grown in very tight places. If you have more room, think about starting a proper school orchard. You will have to get the approval of the head teacher and the formal permission of the landowner, which is most likely to be a local authority, but often these are not too difficult to obtain. The Fruitful Schools project, which is part of the Commonwealth Orchard, is your first port of call for information about, and support for, any school orchard idea. This can be found online at http://www.commonwealthorchard.com.

Schools in country districts often have more land. If you want to see your children's playground burgeoning with wildlife and educational opportunities, get talking to people. A group of parents can easily persuade most head teachers of the desirability of such a project. As suggested above, charities like Scottish Native Woods and Borders Forest Trust, or the Community Woodland Association, are really worth consulting. They may want to take up your idea and lead a project, or they may be able to support you in doing so. Either way, they will have the expertise to make sure that it is done well.

Fi Martynoga

SPECIES, SPACING & SPACES

So you'd like to plant trees? The right tree in the right place, for the right reasons? Like everything else worth doing, it's worthwhile spending the time to do it right. Of course, nature can plant trees herself, so why not leave her to it?

Establishing woodlands through natural regeneration is cheaper and easier than collecting the seed, storing it, sowing it out to seed beds, germinating it, selecting the seedlings, planting them out, undercutting them to produce a good root system for transplanting, keeping them free from pests and diseases, lifting them, bagging them up, doing the paperwork, transporting them to the tree planting site and planting them, isn't it?

So, why not let nature take the strain every time? We do regenerate woods in this way in the UK, and other countries rely upon it even more. The problem is that we mostly don't have the right trees in the right place to take advantage of nature's fecundity. We live in a deforested landscape and there may not be mother trees nearby to provide seed. The mother trees may be of species we don't particularly want, or their genetic quality may be poor or adapted to another place. The ground may be covered in a thick mat of vegetation that the seeds can't penetrate. If the landscape was a fully functioning wildwood, it would easily replenish itself, but we are a very long way from that.

The golden rule for natural regeneration seems to be that when you want it, you don't get it, and when you don't want it, that's when the ground is soon bristling with young seedlings!

So, often we have to plant. We know a lot about the characteristics of tree species, their sensitivities, their growth habits, their qualities. This handbook brings a lot of that hard-earned knowledge together in one place. We need to make careful choices. Which is the right tree in the right place and what are the right reasons? The variables are listed and discussed below.

The right reasons

We plant trees for many different reasons, all of them right for their particular situation. The beauty of tree planting is that you can often achieve multiple objectives. The most common benefits are biodiversity, timber, fuel wood, wild harvest, shelter, landscape, recreation, amenity, field sports and education. It is seldom, but it does sometimes happen, that woodland management objectives clash with one another – for example, dynamic forms of recreation and sensitive species of wildlife in one place. Hunting and shooting come to mind.

Whatever the objectives, it is essential to list them in order of priority. This gives a good steer to the person selecting the tree species and the pattern in which they will be planted. In fact, all the other decisions flow from this ranking exercise, only constrained by the limitations of the site. The key considerations for each objective are now simply listed below:

- **biodiversity** - mainly native species, variable spacing, other habitats;

- **timber** - softwood/hardwood timber species, good fit to site;

- **fuel wood** - fuel wood system, e.g. thinnings or coppice;

- **wild harvest** - mainly native species, shrubs, ground flora;

- **shelter** – wind-permeable shelter strips, narrow features;

- **landscape** - natural or cultural 'sense of place';

- **recreation** - roads and tracks, trees as a matrix;

- **amenity** - internal woodland landscape, access through the woods;

- **field sports** - habitat for pheasants and other game birds, flighting areas;

- **education** - access, outdoor classrooms.

Soils

The soil is the major constraint to the choice of tree to be planted. The best land is usually reserved for agriculture, to grow food. Forestry has to make do with land marginal to this, either on a small scale with shelter strips in arable country, or in larger areas in the uplands. The best soil is a deep, freely draining 'brown earth' with plenty of organic material. Poorer soils are shallower, or wetter, or rockier, or lower in nutrients, or more acidic, or, if you're unlucky, all of these. Only a few species grow well in a combination of these factors. Step forwards Sitka spruce. Its ability to thrive on poor, wet, acidic soils in the uplands is why this one species now accounts for more than half of all the trees in Scottish woods and forests. Understanding soils is a science in itself, but a lot can be gleaned from soil maps produced by the Soil Survey of Scotland. Someone will have to dig some soil pits and have a good look at what is under the surface.

Climate

As you rise up a hill, so the weather becomes more extreme: temperatures drop, wind speed increases, snow lies longer. Temperatures can also drop to extremes in frost hollows in the lowlands. Winds can be funnelled around and inbetween hills. Exposed coastal locations suffer from salt spray. Species have their preferences. Ash doesn't like frost. Sycamore and alder can tolerate wind. Corsican pine can tolerate coastal locations.

Climate change

We know the climate is changing, but we can't predict exactly what that is going to mean for forestry. Some species, like beech and hornbeam, native to southern Britain may do even better in Scotland. Others may decline due to pests and diseases. There seem to be a lot of forest pathogens around at present. The best advice is probably to spread the risk. Plant mixed woodlands and if one species fails, there will be a natural resilience. The more diverse the ecosystem, the more stable it tends to be.

Geographical area

The climate and soils become a little tougher as you travel northwards but altitude has a greater effect. It's windier on the coast and the temperatures are more extreme in the middle of the country: places like Altnaharra, Braemar and Eskdalemuir often record the highest and lowest temperatures. What is very noticeable is that the west of Scotland is wetter than the east. May and June sometimes pass with barely a drop of rain in the east of Scotland. This means that trees tolerant of wet soils, like willow and downy birch, will thrive in the west, and trees tolerant of drought, like Scots pine, will do better in the east. The profiles of species in this book will further guide you in the choice of trees likely to thrive in your area. It is also important in the east of Scotland to get all your trees planted early before any drought takes effect.

Scale

Obviously, the bigger, the better from the biodiversity, timber and fuel wood production points of view. Also many forms of recreation – mountain biking, orienteering, horse riding – need a reasonable-sized woodland to work best. However, the most effective shelter-belts are narrow, and a school wood can be very small and still valuable.

How you protect your trees from pests also depends upon scale. In large upland forests, deer culling is the preferred option. Medium-sized woodlands can be fenced against deer, stock and rabbits. In small woods that are under a hectare in area, or irregular woods, individual protection using tree shelters or spiral guards can be most cost effective.

Growth rates and spacing

Growing trees together in a woodland is a trade-off between timber quality and growth rate. Plant the trees widely and they will grow quickly, but with big branches and tapering trunks – which won't matter if you're not hoping to get timber from them. Three-metre spacing, which is very common, is now considered to be a bit too wide for timber, without heavy pruning. If the trees are planted at less than 2-metre spacing, they will grow straighter, taller, more columnar and with smaller branches. Some species, such as the spruces, are able to thin themselves through vigorous competition. Others, such as the larches, will slow down and almost stop growing altogether. The faster you grow the trees, the sooner they can be harvested, the money put back into the woodlands, and the next generation of trees established. If the timber is used for long-lasting products, then the carbon that the trees have sequestered during their lifetimes is kept locked up for a long time.

Pests and diseases

The range of organisms that rely on trees for sustenance is staggering. They range from large mammals such as red deer to bacteria, such as that which causes acute oak decline. Oak trees alone have several hundred species partial to snacking on it and have developed a survival strategy that involves producing a second flush of growth, known as lammas growth (see page 179).

Mixtures

Scotland's natural forest is special. The northern upland part of Scotland is part of the mainly coniferous boreal forest which stretches round the world. Southern and lowland Scotland are part of the once equally extensive mainly broadleaved temperate forest. The west coast is so wet and windy that it's called an oceanic forest. These forest zones affect the way you plant your trees.

In the uplands, the scale is outsized and the forest structure is simpler. It's fine to have largish areas of pine, spruce, fir and birch. On the lower ground and in the lowlands then the scale becomes smaller. It's good practice to plant 12 to 20 trees of the same species in a group. This enables slower growing species like oak and beech to grow at their own rate and not to be outgrown by faster growing trees such as sycamore or spruce. 12 to 20 planted trees will be reduced through natural mortality or thinning to just 2 or 3 mature trees, leading to a very diverse woodland.

If you want to grow timber, the very best way is to use a slightly faster growing nurse species. This provides upward growth, encouraging all the trees in the stand to grow upwards rather than outwards. The nurse trees can be removed gradually through thinning leaving a stand of high quality timber trees. Suitable mixtures are oak and Scots pine, ash with larch or more complex mixtures.

Silviculture

Once the trees are planted, the job isn't finished. Some mortality is normal and further 'beating up' planting may be required to get the plantation up to full stocking. Weed competition may be a real problem in the lowlands and can be tackled through cultivation, cutting, mulching or herbicides. Once the woodland is established then the silviculture, the tending of the woods, begins. Tree shelters, fences, ditches and tracks need to be maintained. Pests need to be controlled. Trees may need to be pruned to improve quality and thinned to steer the woodland towards its optimum balance of trees to achieve all of the benefits it can deliver. Forestry is an art as well as a science and tree planting represents the first steps of a long and delightful journey. Few things are more worthwhile and satisfying than planting trees.

Donald McPhillimy

NO-FENCE PLANTING

No-fence planting (NFP) is an innovative approach to tree establishment in areas where overgrazing by large herbivores is limiting natural regeneration.

The term NFP comprises several different planting methods that have been developed by Steve Watson and the organisation he founded in 1985, Tree Shepherds. The techniques are derived from a study of the natural processes by which self-sown trees have managed to survive in the Welsh uplands, despite intense grazing pressure by sheep and cattle.

Although native woodland now covers only 3–5 per cent of Snowdonia, the vast majority of the trees are self-sown and have established under severe grazing pressure. Using volunteer labour, Steve and Tree Shepherds began to experiment in finding ways to mimic the processes by which these trees were able to survive.

By studying self-sown trees on overgrazed land, including young, establishing, and mature ones, Steve was able to identify the types of micro-sites where survival was possible. By 1997 many thousands of 'no-fence-planted' trees were well established at dozens of heavily grazed sites in Snowdonia.

In 2000 Tree Shepherds registered as a charity. In this same year the various NFP methods became grant-aided within the Welsh agri-environment scheme 'Tir Gofal'. NFP has recently been incorporated into the new Welsh agri-environment scheme 'Glastir'.

Tree Shepherds only plant trees on grazed farmland, but without the need for:

- any protective fencing;
- removal or reduction of livestock;
- loss of grazing;
- change of land use.

No-fence planted woodlands retain their agricultural land usage, and therefore still qualify for subsidy payments under the IAC's quotas.

By 2010 Tree Shepherds had established trees at more than 100 heavily grazed sites in north Wales. Since 2009 NFP trial sites have been established in Yorkshire, the Scottish Borders, and on the Isle of Arran. NFP is not intended as a replacement to the traditional fenced and stock-excluded planting methods, but rather, as a pragmatic approach to the establishment of tree cover in those areas in which it would otherwise be quite impossible.

There are a number of potential applications for NFP, particularly in upland situations where trees are wanted and it is not possible or desirable to reduce impacts from livestock. The following applications are of particular relevance:

- Where a new generation of trees is needed in an ancient wood pasture, but it is important to continue grazing.

- In remnant fragments of native woodland on burns and riversides where younger age classes of tree are absent due to the lack of safe niches for natural regeneration.

- On hillsides of dense bracken and gorse (or even broom) where low-density tree cover is desirable. The presence of gorse or broom also enables tree establishment on non-sloping land.

- Across treeless landscapes where a reduction in grazing pressure may take place in the future and it is desirable to 'inoculate' the landscape with seed sources.

- To enhance landscapes with large, crowned, open-grown trees.

- To provide future habitat for rare epiphytes (plants growing on the boles and branches of trees), where these occur on isolated open-grown trees.

- To safeguard rare tree species in situ where reduction in livestock numbers is not possible.

- To supplement existing regeneration with additional species, such as oak, which tend to be absent because they are preferentially browsed.

- To enhance or create woodland corridors (riparian or otherwise) to link remnant woodlands and populations.

- To plant on the outside of existing fenced schemes so as to soften the straight-lined woodland edge of the latter.

Producing planting stock

The majority of plants used in NFP are collected as self–sown seedlings through May and June, at the first leaf stage, from sites where they would normally be lost to browsing. Every effort is made to collect seedlings from the same valley as the planting site. These recently germinated seedlings are transported from their site in water before being transferred to pots in local nurseries, and kept shaded for several weeks. Some seedlings, especially alder, can reach 30cm by the end of their first growing season. Relatively large plants (minimum 1.2m tall) are generally needed for NFP techniques, and Tree Shepherds can produce hardened-off, 1.2m-tall, pot-grown whips by the end of the second growing season. Due to the extremely rocky nature of most upland sites it is necessary to use pot-grown plants.

Bare-rooted stock can be used only where the soil quality is good enough, and only for some of the NFP methods. Seedlings can be lined out in a nursery bed to produce whips, again by the end of their second season. The main benefits of using bare rooted stock are reduced labour costs at the nursery, and lightness, making transport to the planting site easier.

The collection of self-sown seedlings from sites that are either too shaded or overgrazed for their survival is advantageous in that this stock has already undergone a natural selection process, and, as a result, early-years losses are reduced. This method is also ideal for a community nursery set-up. Communal seedling collection is a great way for people to get to know each other, and even at the end of the first day, tangible results can be seen.

It is only cost-effective to collect such seedlings from sites where they occur in profusion. Holly, hawthorn and rowan seedlings are likely to be found directly beneath the parent trees; alder seedlings are found alongside burns and river edges or in mossy sites, from June onwards. Oak saplings are grown from seed as they do not lift well at this stage. It is important to take only seedlings in their first year, because once they have become woody, an almost bonsai habit can set in, with slow growth over-extending the time they must be kept in the nursery to gain the necessary stem-length.

The planting techniques

The key to keeping grazing animals away from young trees is to reduce their accessibility and visibility. Many species, including rowan and ash, have evolved to grow a single, straight and unbranched stem in their first few seasons (even if in open aspects with no shade). By this habit they are positioning vulnerable leading shoots beyond the reach of grazing and browsing animals in as short a time as possible, and using the minimum resources. The sabre-planting and gorse-planting methods detailed below imitate the different ways in which a wild tree might naturally escape being eaten. Whilst a naturally regenerated seedling may be progressively browsed and might, if lucky enough to be in a suitable micro-site, eventually survive, NFP bypasses this prolonged process and allows quick and reliable establishment.

Trees must be at least 1.2m tall at planting, whereas the self-sown trees must survive from tiny seedlings. Careful selection of micro-sites can extend the range where establishment might occur naturally. This means sabre-planting can be carried out on less steep slopes than those where natural sabre-shaped trees might be found.

No-fence planting in Scotland

The work done in Wales has resulted in a large number of trees becoming successfully established within land that is grazed to varying degrees, mostly by sheep, but in some cases, also by wild goats, cattle and a small deer population. To find out whether NFP trees could cope with the heavier impact of Scotland's deer, the techniques had to be put to the test again in Scotland. An opportunity eventually arose in the summer of 2010 when the authors planted 30 trees around Traquair, in the Borders. These were ash and sessile oak, with a few downy birch and alder, most of them sabre-planted, although some – on gentle slopes – were planted within gorse. The trees were roughly 1.1 to 1.4m tall, in 17.5cm pots. Planting locations were all grazed and browsed by sheep, roe deer and in one case, horses, with sika deer present in the higher elevation sites.

Sabre planting

Sabre planting mimics the semi-recumbent trees, found on steep slopes and riverbanks, that have swept and tapered bases, formed by evading browsing through gradual stem extension out and over the slope.

Sabre planting uses pot-grown trees at least 1.2m in height, planted at an angle on steep banks, or at the topmost and outer edges of landfalls and unconformities. Trees are pruned to remove lower side-shoots and branches, and protected at the base by a spiral guard. This technique is enhanced if the planting position is within a certain amount of cover, for example, surrounded by gorse, broom, bracken, or bramble. However, if the slope is particularly steep and/or the tree species is less palatable (such as alder, hawthorn, or blackthorn), this is not essential.

Local farmers were happy to accept the planting of a few trees once they understood what was involved. Sites with moderate to steep banks and some field layer or scrub cover were chosen. Within this, a short crowbar was used to break up the soil, ready to be dug out with a rabbiting spade. Great care was taken to avoid disturbing the lower edge of the hole and, whilst digging, soil was gathered onto a sack. Once the hole was dug, the tree was taken out of the plastic pot and placed in the hole, then the carefully conserved soil was tipped from the sack and the tree firmed in with the boot heel. It's important not to lever downwards and loosen the bottom edge of the hole, as this must be firm so as to support the leaning stem and rootball until roots establish. The soil was dry due to the season of planting, so each tree received a can of water. This wouldn't be necessary if planting was carried out before the growing season. A spiral guard was attached to the bottom of the tree to avoid bark stripping, and lower branches were pruned off to limit the attractiveness and visibility of the tree to large herbivores.

Certain species, like oak and Scots pine, can straighten up too quickly for this method to work – before the stem is long enough for leading shoots to emerge only within the safety zone. When working with such trees, the planting angle should be exaggerated in order to slow this premature straightening.

Browsing-induced sabre habit is a global phenomenon in trees. Natural examples can be observed, in their millions, in every county of the UK on steep slopes and riverbanks. All tree species, if tolerant of browsing, appear to be able to adopt this habit. In Scotland, where red deer predominate, as in Glen Coe, these naturally occurring sabre trees are only to be seen on slopes of 60° angles or steeper, or else along the top edges of steeper, almost vertical landfalls. For land grazed by sheep, the micro-sites are on slopes of at least 45° in angle. At such Scottish sites, sabre-planting will need to be a roped-access activity. In red deer country, stock plants will need to be shorter and there must be an acceptance of gradual sabre-habit formation through browsing pressure. It is hoped that more Scottish trials, specifically in red deer areas, can be carried out in the near future.

Gorse planting

This technique is often used in combination with sabre-planting if a slope is present. However, gorse-planting is not dependent upon sloping ground, but merely the presence of gorse. With its spiky and unpalatable twigs, gorse not only physically dissuades browsers but also hides new trees amongst its vegetation.

Young Scots pine trees in particular are wonderfully camouflaged amongst gorse, or broom, wherever clumps are thick enough. A little determination is required to push through thickets of gorse to find a suitable planting site: being a tree fanatic helps! Stout trousers and gloves are required, as well as a good pruning saw, such as a Silky. This can be used to cut a path into the planting site, cut material from bushes elsewhere to block the access of livestock and deer, and, with care, to prune gorse stems from around the branches of the planted tree to avoid abrasion during strong winds. A short rope can be used to tie back gorse stems to facilitate planting. The tied-back branches can then be released, so that they spring back and provide cover. The hole for a pot-grown tree is prepared in the same way as for sabre planting, and a spiral guard should be used to avoid bark stripping by rabbits.

Gorse-planted and sabre-planted trees should be planted a little deeper (3 to 6cm) so as to counter any pot-grown root-cramping. With both techniques, it is necessary to scrape back any bracken or gorse litter prior to digging. This is particularly important when planting during dry weather, as dry litter, if included in the in-fill, could cause desiccation. Such litter should be replaced at the very last, as a top-mulch.

Giant willow cuttings

In Wales, Steve Watson has had great success in establishing large (3m or bigger) grey willow *(Salix caprea x cinerea)* in wet areas on grazed land. Stems are left intact, with branches, twigs, and buds. The below-ground portion is pruned at planting so as to be at least 50 to 60cm in length and so as to place the lowest branching fork just below the surface. This offers greater wind stability in the period before rooting has occurred.

Success?

At the time of writing (February 2011), all trees have survived, 70 per cent have been unbrowsed, 25 per cent have been moderately browsed, and 5 per cent have been heavily browsed after a severe winter. I look forward to seeing these native trees flourish in the Borders where so little native woodland remains, and each newly planted tree makes an important contribution to habitat restoration.

Richard Thompson
has worked for Forest Research and is currently Native Woodlands Officer for Forest Enterprise.

Steve Watson
is the founder of Tree Shepherds.

COLLECTING SEED FROM TREES & SHRUBS

It may seem a slow way to start, but there are huge advantages in beginning at the very beginning and growing your own trees and shrubs from seed. Of course, you can buy them, and those wanting just a few specimen trees may want to do this. Seedlings are available as cell-grown (in clever root-training containers that open out so that you can remove the plants easily), bare-rooted, or container-grown specimens.

The last of these, the container-grown seedlings, are the most expensive. All bought seedlings will cost more than trees raised in your own nursery from seed collected within your locality. However, it is worth mentioning these categories of commercially available stock, as anyone contemplating very large-scale planting may want to consider supplying a nursery with seed they have collected and getting them to grow them on contract. In this way a tree-planting project (or business) can ensure stock of the right origins, in the right quantities, ready at the right time, without all the problems of hunting around in a hurry. This approach has been successfully adopted by some large environmental restoration projects, notably at Carrifran Wildwood.

Origin and provenance

It stands to reason that an oak raised from seed collected in southern or eastern Europe may be hard pushed to flourish in a Highland glen. Until the great revival of interest in native trees, which started thirty or more years ago, however, much nursery stock had precisely such origins. In seed collecting terms, 'origin' refers to the genetic composition (the genotype) of the trees from which the seed is collected, which is taken to be adapted to the particular environmental conditions of that site. 'Provenance' refers more simply to the site at which the parent tree was growing. Thus Scots pine seedlings of Deeside provenance might actually be of German origin, if that Deeside plantation had been grown from German stock. So be on your toes when planning to collect seed, and consider the possible origins of parent trees, especially when they are growing within estate policies. The wilder the situation, the more likely the tree is to be native. Even then you can be mistaken, so follow the Forestry Commission guidelines explained by Rick Worrell in 'Seed Provenance and the Law' (pages 67 to 71).

For the amateur tree grower or small nursery, seed collecting is very much part of the fun and interest of growing trees. Great importance is attached to knowing the precise origins of each bed of trees. Such work can make an important contribution to the conservation of our native forest gene pool, and you will be planting a well-adapted tree.

Methods of seed collecting

Commercial methods of tree seed collection can involve tree felling, hydraulic hoists, tarpaulins and several other techniques. For the small-scale and amateur seed collector in Scotland, equipment is minimal: a 3-litre plastic tub carried on an improvised string 'handle', a rucksack containing a few cloth or polythene bags for separating the different species (but beware of the seed sweating in plastic bags), an identification book, and labels. A long stick with a hook can be useful for bending branches down towards you, or you can use a custom designed high-pruner. Wherever possible, though, cutting of any part of the tree should be avoided. Ample seed is nearly always available from accessible branches, though Scots pine can prove frustrating in this respect because there are usually relatively few cones at low levels. Always drop a label into the bag of collected seed stating the date collected, precise location and species.

Damaged limbs and recently fallen trees often produce prolific seed, and it is tempting to home in on these and collect a great deal from them. The ease of doing so must be balanced against the narrowing of genetic variation in the seedlings produced. It can also be argued that the seed collector should be looking for particular attributes of form rather than simply what is easiest and quickest to collect. This is clearly of most concern where the trees to be grown are destined for the timber market. A main objective when collecting seed of native trees, however, is to secure seed from truly 'wild' individuals and not from planted trees which, though of native species, may well be of foreign origin. You should therefore avoid the vicinity of gardens, lodges and estate houses where ornamental planting has taken place in the past. Seek out instead the banks of rivers, gullies in the hills and the more remote woods.

A couple of other poor practices are collecting from isolated trees, which are often self-pollinated and produce seed of low viability; and from areas where hybridisation occurs between species (notably downy and silver birch in Scotland), producing stock of indistinct species.

Deciding how much to collect will clearly depend on how many trees you wish to grow, and it is worth consulting the species guides to see what weight of seed will provide a suitable number of seedlings. Such figures should be treated as guidelines only, as viability differs quite widely from area to area and from year to year.

Timing of seed collection

The time for seed collection is between the moment it ripens and the time when it disperses. This window varies greatly from species to species. It may be a few days, as in aspen, to several weeks, as in dog rose, for example. Gales, hungry insects, birds and mammals all conspire to reduce the size of that window greatly. Timing collections accurately will make a big difference to the efficiency of the operation. If you time it too late, many seeds will already have dispersed, but if you're too early, seed with low viability may be inadvertently collected: the first acorns and hazelnuts to drop are usually malformed or empty. It helps, of course, if an eye can be kept on your selected seed trees and the progress of fruit ripening.

In every season of the year there is some collecting of native tree and shrub seed to be carried out (see the seed calendar on page 66). Willows may catch you out by seeding soon after bud break, their fluffy seed being quite quickly blown away on the wind. Birch is easiest to collect green from August onwards. Rowan and hawthorn berries will be ripening in September; alder cones should be collected in October or November but, like birch, can be scavenged in the new year. Scots pinecones can be collected in January or February or can wait into March or April before the spring warmth starts to open them out and disperse the seed within. Ash and elm can be collected green in the summer or left until brown, sometime in the winter.

An early spring and/or a hot dry summer will bring forward seeding time; poor weather, the reverse. Seed of a given species will often ripen earlier in the south of the country than in the north, and this effect can even be discerned on the north and south sides of a single glen, where the aspect affects ripening time.

The periodicity of seeding is different from species to species as well as among trees of the same species and even from year to year in the same individual tree. Often a heavy-seed year is followed by a poor one. Birch is one of the few native species that seems to produce well every year. Weather will clearly have a considerable influence. Rains will inhibit insect pollination, late frosts can kill embryo fruits, drought or cold can cause seed abortion and strong winds can destroy flowers at any time, to give just a few examples.

Different species reach flowering age at different ages: birch and other pioneers as early as six to seven years, sessile oak at nearer 40 years. There is usually a particularly fruitful period of life just after vegetative growth has slowed during middle age. Such facts become part of the experienced seed collector's general knowledge, becoming as important in efficient collecting as detailed local knowledge on individual trees of good form that offer accessible and usually fecund branches.

The ethics and law of seed collecting

In Scottish law, it is worth remembering that the seed on a tree belongs, like the tree itself, to the person on whose land it is growing. Even collecting a few handfuls of birch or alder seed from a remote Highland glen is, strictly speaking, against the law. Contrast this with the Nordic countries where 'everyone's right' enables you to collect wild fruit and berries, within certain limitations, regardless of who owns the land. However, in many cases you will have no trouble gaining permission, as few people value tree seed. In the case of Scots pine, however, most native Caledonian sources are now being used for commercial or conservation purposes and you should definitely not collect from these without permission. You should also take particular care to seek permission on nature reserves and on Sites of Special Scientific Interest (SSSIs), which may be managed for natural regeneration.

Leaving 'some for the wee beasties' is a good general rule when collecting seed. Again, it is hard to make any impact when collecting the light seeds of birch and alder, but when picking wild cherries, holly or elder berries it is something you should remember. In many situations, by collecting only what you can reach by standing on your toes you will cause little or no damage.

If you intend to grow your seed into trees for use in FC grant-aided schemes, in the case of oak, aspen, beech and some other broadleaved trees, as well as the conifers including Scots pine, then the whole process is regulated by European regulations. This subject is covered in the chapter on provenance by Dr Rick Worrell (pages 67 to 71). So long as seed is solely for your own use, such matters need not worry you. Although much seed is imported commercially from abroad, there are laws against bringing any plant seed into the UK without a licence. As much as anything, this is to help prevent the movement of disease and pests.

The Original Editorial Team: Bernard & Emma Planterose, Martin Howard & Ron Greer

SEED
TREATMENT
& STORAGE

This chapter looks at the different ways you can store seed and treat it so that it is ready for sowing. It deals predominantly with the seed of native trees and shrubs, though many of the principles discussed apply to other species too.

Principles

Seeds come in many shapes and sizes. They may be succulent (like berries and drupes) or dry (nuts, winged seeds and so on), and there is a corresponding variety of storage and pre-germination treatments practised by nurseries.

In nature, seed usually remains dormant until conditions – moisture, temperature, oxygen and light – are right. It may be beneficial that some of a seed crop germinates the first spring and some the following spring. This may depend on a growth inhibitor disappearing, such as a bird eating the flesh of a berry, or weathering causing the breakdown of a hard seed coat, or on the stimulation of a growth promoter, such as a temperature rise after a period of cold.

But in the nursery situation we need to achieve relatively even germination in space and time, and maximum germination from the seed that has been painstakingly collected. We may also need to have seed in store to provide for the poor seed years, a natural hazard of using local seed sources.

Germination can be artificially hastened by treatment involving temperature changes and or physical removal of flesh or seed coats. Such treatments may also increase germination percentage. It's simpler to let time and natural processes do their work in an environment of suitable temperature and moisture conditions along with security from predators. This process, known as stratification, is sometimes the only treatment applied to a seedlot, and is sometimes combined with another treatment, such as maceration.

Whilst the majority of seeds have to go through a period of dormancy, those of a few species do not and must be sown immediately. Examples include willows and aspen.

Careful labelling with details of weight, dates and treatment ensure that the information needed at sowing will be there. You should take account of the purity of the seed when weighing. Is it 'clean', or 'dirty' – with scales, wings, flesh, stalks or leaves?

Stratification

Whether or not you are trying to accelerate breaking of dormancy, the technique of stratification is central. Its aim is to provide an ideal environment for seed to ripen or break dormancy, and the methods are essentially very simple, depending on the scale of the operation and personal preference.

Containers can vary from margarine tubs and small plant pots through fish boxes and barrels to purpose-built cold-frame constructions for large quantities. Seed ('dirty' or 'clean') is mixed with coarse sand in roughly equal volumes. Mixtures of sand, peat, ground bark and leaf mould are alternatives you could try. Exposure to the rain and outside ambient temperatures, aeration, complete protection from predators and free drainage of water through the seed-sand mixture are all conditions that must be achieved. For many small native nurseries, the fish-box method will be adequate. You will need lots of good plastic fish boxes (with holes in the bottom), the smallest gauge wire mesh (or doubled-up layers of 1.5cm gauge), plus trestles or logs to raise the boxes out of the reach of rodents. In low rainfall areas, open stratifying containers may need to be watered.

Once up and running, there may seem little need to bother with intensive methods of breaking dormancy, as a supply of stratified seed is established from seed collected a season or two before. Hiccups in supply due to bad seed years may occasionally need to be overcome by acceleration techniques from time to time.

Physical separation

Certain species will require separation of seeds from seed cases, just for easier storage and sowing.

The winged seed of conifers held in a cone is a clear example of where the seed needs to be physically extracted from its natural container. On the tree, the cones usually dry out, the scales open and the seed is taken by the wind as it is released, over the course of several weeks, or even months.

For large-scale extraction, cones are generally dried on grids in kilns and mechanically agitated to help release the seed. The temperature in the kiln starts at about 30°C and can be taken up to about 60°C, the whole process taking about one week. At a smaller scale, pinecones can be heated in trays over a radiator or woodstove or in an airing cupboard and shaken vigorously in a tightly lidded container such as a large plastic tub.

Alder seed is also held in cones, which again need to dry out before the seed is released. In the small nursery situation, alder cones can be dried in a warm room in the autumn when they are picked, perhaps hanging from the ceiling in sheets or pillowcases. These can then be beaten with a rolling pin to release the seed, which can be sieved through a large vegetable steamer. A vigorous beating will cause the cones themselves to disintegrate, but the resulting dust does no harm to the seed in storage – though it needs to be accounted for in weight calculations on sowing.

Gorse seed is prickly to extract so, if possible, cut small branches laden with seeds and hang to dry in sheets in a very warm room. The pods pop open and seed can be sieved out. Otherwise pick pods and leave them in a closed container to open. Seed left in pods too long is often entirely consumed by insect larvae.

Physical separation of seed from succulent fruit is a good way to get to know your seeds intimately but it is time consuming and requires further 'apparatus'. The 'after-ripening' period of one or more winters which these seeds need can be reduced to one winter in some cases by removing the inhibitory fleshy covering, and germination percentages may be increased in the case of species where dormancy only lasts one winter.

Succulent seed includes that of rowan, whitebeam, hawthorn, sloe, guelder rose, elder, cherries, roses, holly and yew. The flesh of these will eventually rot in stratification but can, if desired, be separated from the seed by maceration and water washes. This can be achieved in a number of ways according to individual preferences, but whichever way you choose, it is easier if the flesh is allowed to rot a bit in a plastic bag in a cool place beforehand. Rubbing small quantities on a hard surface with a block of wood, trampling in the bath tub, or a short burst of the slow speed on a food liquidiser or blender can give effective maceration.

Either way, the viable seed is usually separated from the resulting mash by floating the latter off in a bucket or tank of water, but the whole lot could then be consigned to the stratification box.

Temperature treatments

Warm and cold treatment is a relatively exacting procedure compared with stratification and at minimum requires access to a fridge and heated room. All seeds in berries require separation before such treatment.

The cold part of the treatment usually involves a period at 3 to 5°C, which can be achieved in the main compartment of a normal fridge. The warm part usually involves a period of between 20 and 30°C, such as can be found in an airing cupboard. On a large scale, insulated walk-in containers that can be heated or cooled are used.

Species that can be treated in this way include hawthorn, cherry, rowan, ash and holly. The detailed information required can be found in the Forestry Commission's *Seed Manual for Ornamental Trees and Shrubs*.

Dry storage

Some seed, such as that of pine, birch and alder, can be stored in sealed plastic bags for quite long periods, which may help overcome the irregularity of supplies from nature. Their moisture content must be reduced to below 10 per cent (as it would be after the drying process in a warm room) and their temperature kept between 3 and 5°C. Note that so-called 'recalcitrant' seeds such as acorns cannot withstand moisture loss and are therefore killed by this treatment. These can be mixed with moist leaves, hung in a plastic bag in a cool, dry place and checked occasionally for drying out.

Several other species can be stored cool and dry over the winter, including pine, birch, alder, hazel, beech, oak, gorse and broom. These conditions can be provided quite easily in Scotland in nursery and garden sheds or in garages, provided that containers are kept away from rodents and other seed predators. Hessian or plastic bags (watch out for rotting!) hung from ceilings and lidded tubs can all be used.

SPECIES TABLE

Species	Storage and Treatment Notes
Alder (Alnus glutinosa)	Dry cones and extract seed by vigorous agitation. Store cool and dry. Optional stratification two months before sowing.
Ash (Fraxinus excelsior)	Seed embryo requires further time to develop fully, so stratify in sand for two winters. Do not attempt to separate seed from wing.
Aspen (Populus tremula)	Not possible to store.
Beech (Fagus sylvatica)	Store dry and cool, turning occasionally; OR store at -5°C; OR store dry to mid-February and then stratify for three weeks before sowing.

Species	Storage and Treatment Notes
Birch *(Betula spp.)*	Spread catkins out in a cool place to dry. Store in fridge until sowing. Optional stratification for two to three months before sowing.
Blackthorn/sloe *(Prunus spinosa)*	Stratify in sand for two winters.
Broom *(Cytisus scoparius)*	Pop the pods open in sheets or lidded containers in a warm place. Sieve seed and store dry until required. Put seed in a bowl and pour on water just after boiling, then leave to cool, strain and sow.
Bird cherry and wild cherry (Gean) *(Prunus spp.)*	Stratify in sand for one winter.
Elder *(Sambucus nigra)*	Stratify in sand for one winter.
Wych elm *(Ulmus glabra)*	Often sown directly after collection but can be dried and stored for several years until required.
Gorse/Whin *(Ulex europaeus)*	Treat as for broom, above.
Guelder rose *(Viburnum opulus)*	Stratify in sand for one winter; OR remove flesh from seed and sow immediately.
Hawthorn *(Crataegus monogyna)*	Stratify in sand for two winters; OR hot and cold treatment: 20 to 30°C to new year followed by 1 to 5°C until spring sowing.

Species	Storage and Treatment Notes
Hazel (*Corylus avellana*)	Immerse in water and discard any nuts that float. Stratify in sand for one winter; OR store cool and dry.
Holly (*Ilex aquifolium*)	Stratify whole for two winters; OR separate flesh from seed and stratify for one winter. The seed begins to germinate in the second winter so take care to watch out for this. Further germination occurs in third winter/spring.
Juniper (*Juniperus communis*)	Stratify for one winter. Some seed takes two to three years to germinate, however.
Oak (*Quercus spp.*)	Immerse in water and discard any acorns that float. Store cool and dry or in bags with moist leaves. Moisten with water if signs of drying/shrivelling.
Scots pine (*Pinus sylvestris*)	Extraction by heat in kilns at commercial scale. At small scale, over a radiator. Store in fridge.
Pines, spruce and larches (*Pinus, Picea and Larix spp.*)	Once extracted, these can usually be stored for several years if thoroughly dried to about 6 to 8 per cent moisture and kept at 2 to 5°C. For one winter storage, keep at 2 to 5°C after normal drying. Stratification not required.
Dog rose (*Rosa canina*)	Stratify in sand for two winters; OR remove flesh from seeds and stratify one winter.

Species	Storage and Treatment Notes
Rowan *(Sorbus aucuparia)*	Stratify in sand for one winter; OR remove flesh from seed and stratify for one winter; OR separate seed and keep at 20 to 30°C for two weeks in December, followed by 1 to 5°C from new year until spring sowing.
Sycamore and Norway maple *(Acer spp.)*	Sow immediately; OR store cool and dry then stratify for two months.
Whitebeam *(Sorbus spp.)*	As for rowan.
Willow *(Salix spp.)*	Sow immediately.
Yew *(Taxus baccata)*	Separate flesh (aril) from seed and stratify for two winters; OR stratify whole for two to three winters

The Editorial Team

INVASIVE
ALIEN PESTS
AND PATHOGENS

The past few years have seen unprecedented public concern over the rapid and seemingly unstoppable spread of diseases – mainly imported – that are threatening the health and viability of trees in Scotland and throughout the UK. This chapter examines the origins and effects of the most significant of these diseases, and what we can do individually and collectively to arrest their spread.

The major threats to our forests and woodlands in the twenty-first century

Confirmation of ash dieback, caused by *Chalara fraxinea* (*Hymenoscyphus fraxineus*, formerly called *H. pseudoalbidus*), in October 2012 in East Anglian woodlands generated an explosion of activity in the UK, led largely by keen interest from environmental correspondents in the media. Amongst the varied articles in the newspapers, numerous letters appeared from the public, commenting on and criticising the responses from government. It is not clear why, but the prospect of losing almost all of the UK's ash trees over the next 15 to 20 years generated huge public interest, the like of which is rarely witnessed with environmental problems. The confirmed arrival of *Chalara* was not the first highly damaging invasive alien to arrive in the UK's forests and woodlands. We are currently fighting at least eleven invasive alien problems on our tree populations, most of which entered the UK in this century: there are many others heading our way too, some known, and undoubtedly many unknown.

Dutch elm disease, which killed most UK elms after the aggressive pathogen *Ophiostoma novo-ulmi* entered the UK in the 1960s, is a highly destructive problem that many people will remember. In northern Scotland the disease is still active (*see also* page 133). We know how the pathogen arrived in the UK; we know how the disease spread; we know how incredibly aggressive and damaging the pathogen is. Despite the huge accumulated knowledge from the invasion by *O. novo-ulmi*, any lessons learned from that date apparently were forgotten before the turn of the century. Another elm disease causing concern is elm yellows, caused by a specialised form of bacteria called phytoplasma. Recently, young grafted elm of the new cultivar 'Morfeo' in England were destroyed because of this disease.

A name spoken with trepidation by foresters is *Phytophthora*, which translates as 'plant killer'. We have been aware of these organisms for well over 100 years – potato blight, which resulted in mass starvation and emigration of people from Ireland and western Scotland in the 1840s, is caused by *Phytophthora infestans*. The number of known *Phytophthora*, however, many of which are highly damaging to woody plants, is increasing rapidly. In the UK we have epidemics of *Phytophthora ramorum* killing Japanese larch, and, along with *Phytophthora kernoviae*, damaging many native and ornamental plants. Lawson's cypress and related trees are under attack from *Phytophthora lateralis*. Of particular environmental significance, *Phytophthora austrocedrae* is wiping out juniper in the rare juniper heaths of northern England and Scotland. As an illustration of how puzzling these invasions can be, until the 1990s the only other part of the world where we were aware of *Phytophthora lateralis* was in the native range of *Chamaecyparis lawsoniana*, the Pacific Northwest of North America; in the 1990s, the pathogen was found in France. We also know that *Phytophthora austrocedrae* is present in Chile and Argentina, causing dieback of native *Austrocedrus chilensis*. The highly aggressive and damaging species *Phytophthora cinnamomi* is also widespread in the UK, although damage is largely restricted to ornamental woody plants. Elsewhere this same species is causing immense destruction: in the cork and holm oak-dominated forest communities of the southern Iberian Peninsula, *Phytophthora cinnamomi* threatens the integrity of the ecosystem and the associated cork industry. Oaks elsewhere in Europe are suffering from decline syndromes related to alternating severe drought and waterlogging conditions, combined with infection by various *Phytophthora* species, and attack by bark-boring insects.

Pines are threatened by several problems: pine wood nematode, *Bursaphelenchus xylophilus*, native to North America, is killing pines in Portugal, and has been reported in Spain. Although the relatively cool conditions in Scotland mean that the nematode would not kill pines here, the presence of the organism in timber would have a drastic impact on trade. Pine pitch canker, resulting from infection by *Fusarium circinatum*, however, currently a major problem on plantation radiata pines in north-western Spain, and affecting native shore pine in the same region, is a serious threat to Scots pine. Moreover, in the past 20 years there has been a massive upsurge in defoliation and killing of pines by Dothistroma needle blight in Europe and British Columbia. Recent outbreaks of Dothistroma needle blight, which hitherto was considered a problem in pine plantations in areas of North America and the southern hemisphere, led to the abandonment of Lodgepole and Corsican pines by the Forestry Commission. A combination of these disease problems, coupled with others we have known for many years, present a grave threat to the iconic native Scots pine and should be taken very seriously by the authorities.

Another disease causing concern in England is acute oak decline, which may be caused by bacteria vectored by oak jewel beetles. Acute oak decline has affected mature oaks in the south of England since the 1980s. Both native British oak species, pedunculate and sessile oaks, are susceptible and trees can be killed within four to five years of the onset of symptoms.

Horse chestnut (*Aesculus hippocastanum*) is subject to several destructive pests and pathogens: leaf miner brings what appears to be a very early autumn from the end of July onwards; and bacterial canker, recently arrived in Europe probably from India, kills trees. Horse chestnut is now of little value for use in amenity settings, although other species in the genus *Aesculus* may provide suitable alternatives.

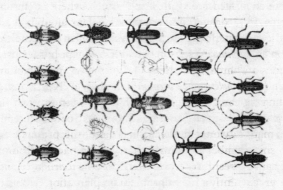

It is not only diseases that are increasing in number and severity. Many alien pest animals are establishing on trees in Europe. Many people might think of mammals in these terms, with, for example, grey squirrels invading our woodlands. It is, however, the influx of exotic invertebrate pests that poses the greatest threat to forests and woodlands. Two species of Asian long-horned beetles, highly destructive wood borers with wide host ranges, have established in various locations in Europe; an outbreak of one species, *Anoplophora glabripennis*, occurred in Kent in early 2012; a vigorous eradication campaign ensued. The ranges of the oak and pine processionary moths are expanding rapidly; oak processionary moth is spreading in south-east England, accompanied by human health problems caused by the irritant hairs shed by the caterpillars. The emerald ash borer has killed some 50–100 million ash trees in North America and is present in continental Europe, in western Russia: it will undoubtedly kill any ash trees that proved tolerant of *Chalara*.

Why are we seeing so many 'new' pests and diseases affecting our trees? Global trade is the main issue: world trade in live plants and in plant products is increasing year on year. Billions of plants are imported into European countries from other continents every year. Major ports in Belgium, the Netherlands and Italy handle huge numbers of these plants, many of which are containerised, meaning that the soil in which they were cultivated in the country of production is included. It is impossible, using current inspection protocols, to determine what microorganisms and, to a large extent, invertebrate pests are present in the soil in the containers or in the plants themselves. Moreover, the use of pesticides by plant producers may mask symptoms of disease, making phytosanitary inspectors' jobs even more futile. From ports of entry, plants go to EU nurseries for growing on before sale to landscapers, forestry and commercial outlets. A serious flaw in the trade system is that, once a plant has entered the EU and got past the limited checks by the phytosanitary authorities, they are treated as if of European origin: it can be very difficult to determine the true source of those plants once within an EU nursery. So far there is no evidence that post-Brexit checking protocols have improved the situation.

Problems associated with climate change certainly exacerbate these problems. Changing environmental conditions impact on both the pest organisms and the host plants, change the dynamics of the interactions, and can lead to greater problems on a wider scale. Recent epidemics of several tree diseases have been linked to increased temperatures. Changes in rainfall patterns will also impact on disease incidence and severity. Increased drought stress will exacerbate certain diseases, whereas outbreaks of other diseases, including Dothistroma needle blight, have been linked to increases in summer rainfall.

It is not clear why ash dieback in particular touched the nation's heart so strongly. The problem did, however, push the campaign for real action forward in the UK, although the authorities were already waking up to the threat posed by invasive alien pests and pathogens. We need comprehensive policies to address the enormous problems of border security against damaging pests and pathogens, which include: increased vigilance at border controls, with improved methods of detection on a mass scale that allow for the huge numbers of plants arriving in EU ports each year; better management of the spread pathways within Europe; and much improvement in public awareness of what they can and should do to help prevent the ecosystem destruction that we already know comes with invasive alien pests and pathogens. There is no room for complacency. The alternatives to strong action are too depressing to contemplate.

Stop the spread

Human activities may not be fully to blame for the spread of all tree pathogens in Scotland, but thoughtless behaviour could certainly contribute to the problem. Both DEFRA and FCS have policies in place to introduce more control to commercial tree importing operations and the movement of certain tree materials around the country. You can look at DEFRA's document *Protecting Plant Health, A Biosecurity Strategy for Great Britain* and see whether you think it measures up to the policies of other countries, New Zealand and Australia, for example.

Both organisations are keen for the public to be informed and aware of tree diseases and pathogens, and like to be told of new observations concerning tree health. When *Chalara fraxinea* was first identified, information fed by the public certainly speeded up the understanding of how far the disease had spread. You can look at the FCS map and see their helpful video about symptoms at:

- http://www.forestry.gov.uk/chalara

You can also observe the few guidelines they recommend to make sure you are not a vector for this, or any other plant disease.

- Stay on the path or trail (dogs, too).

- Brush off loose earth from clothing, footwear, bicycle wheels and dog paws before leaving a site.

- Thoroughly cleanse your footwear, bike tyres and dog's paws once you get home.

- Leave all plant material in the woods where you found it.

The last point may be sad for children who have picked up pretty pine or larch cones, but larch in particular is a great worry, with the south-west of Scotland already having special measures in place to control the ramorum blight, so it is really worth taking the precaution.

If you are purchasing saplings to plant, it is well worth asking the tree nursery about the provenance of the plants (*see* pages 67 to 71). It seems extraordinary that there should ever be imports of ash seedlings, as they germinate so readily and grow like weeds, but it has certainly occurred on a massive scale. Local provenance of native trees, and the more local the better, will give trees a greater chance of succeeding, so refuse to buy imports or 'native' trees grown from foreign seed sources. Similar care with the purchasing of firewood also makes sense.

If you are considering buying saplings and trees, it is always advisable to seek out reputable tree nurseries. Ask them for details about their policies for provenance and the measures they have in place to avoid the spread of tree diseases. Some nurseries will accept seed gathered locally and provide a service for growing on (Alba Trees, for example, propagate nearly all the saplings for Carrifran Wildwood from seeds gathered by volunteers).

Stuart Fraser and Steve Woodward
Professor Stephen Woodward and Research Associate Stuart Fraser, University of Aberdeen, Institute of Biological and Environmental Sciences, Cruickshank Building, Aberdeen AB24 3UU
+44-1224-272669
s.woodward@abdn.ac.uk
www.abdn.ac.uk/ibes/staff/s.woodward

SOWING TREE
& SHRUB SEED

This chapter takes a look at some techniques, for the small-scale grower, for sowing seed and obtaining good germination, concentrating on native species.

Starting out

When we came to sow our first seed I remember getting so bogged down in heavily rotovated sterilised mud and in calculating how many ounces of seed we needed per square yard (and trying to convert that to grams per square metre) for the number of trees we wanted that it was hard to get started. There is plenty of written information on seed sowing, but, as with most things, it's the actual practice that teaches most, especially with the variable germination of locally collected native seed. So this short chapter will, I hope, be a guide through the mire with a few glimmers of the light-footed, economical techniques that evolved at our Duartbeg nursery some years ago.

Basic principles

The seed will most likely have been collected some months before you sow, and stratified or stored in some way since then. It will therefore be in a number of forms: dry; rotted in sand; or perhaps as a sludge in the bottom of a plastic bag. It might be bursting into life already or may still appear to be quite inert. Most seed is sown when the soil is frost-free and warming up in the spring, but some can or should be sown in the autumn. With seeds of species like elm it is optional whether you sow on collection or store them. Others, such as willow and aspen, must be sown directly after collection. See the section 'Seed Treatment and Storage' (pages 44 to 51) for details.

Germination

If the temperature is warm enough, the absorption of water through the seed coat activates the chemical reactions, those growth processes by which the seed embryo produces first the root and then the shoot systems, which eventually rupture the seed coat. Stratification will have softened the seed coat of most hard-coated seeds, but broom and whin benefit from soaking in an equivalent volume of just-boiled water for up to 24 hours before sowing. As germination progresses, the seedling's requirements grow with it: water, oxygen, readily available nutrients and shelter. Remember that the nursery seedbed is an artificial environment, unlike that of the forest clearing where seedlings would grow naturally, and wind is one of the most stressful factors affecting germination.

Seedbeds

Your site will, of course, be ideal – sheltered but not shady or in a frost hollow; slightly sloping to the west; with a powerful, uncontaminated water supply; secure and with good access; light loam; without weed problems – or more likely it has many limitations but is the only land available. For example, the nursery land at Duartbeg, in north-west Sutherland, was only relatively sheltered, on a slightly east-facing slope, had a massive shallow-rooting ash tree at one end and a burn below it that dried up in early summer. Moreover, it was on short-term lease, was swarming with roe deer, had no ready access, and consisted of peat and rocky soil with reeds, iris, bracken and dock. So we tensioned a web windbreak in combination with a deer fence and, within the nursery, sowed strategic windbreak beds of whin and broom, dug a trench between the ash and the nursery to prevent intense root competition, dug a holding pond for pumped irrigation fed by drainage ditches from the nursery, hand-dug and hard-cored tracks and went on and on double-digging to improve the soil. For a site of up to a quarter acre, breaking it in by double-digging is a very good way to get to know your soil. Stones and roots of perennial weeds such as couch grass and dock can be removed and bulky organic fertilisers such as manure incorporated. Free drainage is ensured and seedbeds readily prepared. At Duartbeg we dug a 0.6m-wide trench of whatever length was workable and put the spoil to one side. The compacted bottom of the trench was broken up with spade and pick-axe and stones removed (to make tracks elsewhere). We filled it with as much compost, seaweed or manure as we could afford, then turned the next trench into it, dusted with ground rock phosphate and ground limestone, and kept repeating the process.

Paths and beds were marked out with pegs and string, and we made it a strict rule that the beds were never to be walked on, to avoid compaction. Clods were broken and beds raked level with a long-handled, long-pronged cultivator. The paths became lower as they compacted and could be mulched with sawdust or straw, to deter weeds.

Choosing the width of beds and paths is up to you. It is best to make a bed only twice as wide as you can comfortably reach when weeding, and paths wide enough to take a wheelbarrow. After digging, the beds must be protectively mulched with old, rotting straw until sowing time, when it is raked off. Alternatively, they can be covered with clear polythene, well weighted down, to stimulate an initial germination of weeds, which can then be hoed off before sowing.

This system leaves a light, friable soil from which weeds are easily teased and any excessive rainfall drains; it will have a high organic content and you will have an efficient irrigation system for the whole nursery so that you can keep relatively unconsolidated soil moist. With a different soil you may need to use boards or a roller to press those soil particles together for better capillary action. Get to know your ground and take advice if you need to.

Fertility and mycorrhizas

You can test or have your soil tested for the main nutrients, nitrogen (N), phosphate (P), potassium (K), magnesium (Mg), calcium (Ca) and sulphur (S). The Scottish Agricultural College test of our soil recommended a treatment (with inorganic fertilisers), which we ignored. It was based on an average of several very different soils within the nursery, so we tackled each soil type differently in a rather intuitive way, using, according to availability, unwashed coarse sand, shell-sand, ground limestone, calcified seaweed, fresh seaweed, manure, bracken, comfrey, worm compost, ground rock phosphate, legumes and so on. The soil itself and any plants already growing in it are always fine indicators of its pH and general health. You will have to get to know the weeds so as to distinguish them from young seedling trees and to understand their roles and how to treat them.

The fungal associations of mycorrhizas with particular tree species are very important in the nursery. When a bed of alder seedlings with light-green leaves stuck at 25mm high, we grubbed up some soil and nodules from the roots of mature alders, crumbled them up, sprinkled them on the beds and watered them in. There was no alder within 5km of the nursery, so no Frankia was present in the soil. The leaves turned glossy green and the alders grew 50mm. Likewise when our pine seedlings turned purple we scraped needle litter from the floor of a pinewood and teased it between the seedlings, which rapidly turned dark green and grew strongly. We soon learnt to inoculate any ground that was new to these species.

Sowing

There are various sowing techniques, but the simplest for all except the larger nuts is broadcasting on the soil surface. A moist, not too smooth, seedbed ensures that the seed has good contact with the soil, and a calm day is necessary for sowing light seeds such as birch. We divide the batch of seed roughly in half and sow one side of a bed, then the other side, taking care not to overlap. Scooped by hand from a bucket and sprinkled steadily, with experience you can achieve an even distribution. Seed that has been stratified in sand is sown with its sand, so it is important to know the seed:sand ratio. Density of sowing depends on whether the trees will be lifted after the first growing season or left for a second, in which case they should have more space. We do our sowing by eye, using common sense to tell how close the seeds should be to each other, given that only a proportion of them germinate.

When seeds have already started to germinate, it is more like sowing beansprouts. You have to be very gentle to avoid breaking the sprouted roots and shoots, and aim to cover the seed as soon as possible, but even 75mm sprouts can orientate into trees, albeit with slight 'hockey-stick' roots.

For larger quantities of seed, a wheeled, hand-pulled fertiliser–sand spreader can be adapted to sow tree seed.

All nuts should be buried up to 50mm deep in the soil. We drew a 75 to 100mm-deep drill across the seedbed with a hoe, half filled it with rich compost, sowed the nuts about 25mm apart onto this, then backfilled, before drawing the next drill about 100mm further along. If you plan to undercut rather than transplant you need to think about the arrangement of, and access to, these drills. Undercutting is done with a sharp spade to root-prune *in situ*, stimulating growth of finer roots to give a greater root volume. Oak in particular can have a vigorous taproot, which, given the chance, will keep on going down. This is fine if it's going to stay put, but not so great if you've got thousands of long-rooted transplants to get into the ground.

Willow seed can be sown by cutting branchlets dense with catkins that are just starting to blow. These can be inserted into a moist seedbed, covered with netting (see willow, pages 210 to 218) and kept very humid. The seeds float down and germinate immediately. Treat aspen in the same sort of way.

Covering

Light-coloured, 3-5mm, clean, rounded, neutral grit is best. This will not heat up too much in the sun, blow away, swamp the seed, cake up or affect pH: all factors which affect germination, though variations can of course be used successfully. We could get only 6mm grit (chips) from the nearest quarry, filling our 1.25-tonne trailer for a few pounds, then storing in a weed-free bunker. At sowing time it was barrowed to the seed-bed where we used a scoop (plastic pot) from a bucketful to shake the grit evenly over the seed. This can be a single-handed operation, whereas the shovel and riddle technique needs two pairs of hands. The light seed – birch, alder, bog myrtle – is only just covered, just enough to hold the seed down, create a microclimate and protect from greedy, beady eyes. All other seed can be covered with a layer of grit until the seed is just no longer visible.

Protection

Newly sown and germinating seed is vulnerable to virtually everything – wind, rain, sun, mice, squirrels, birds, weeds – so protecting them has to be a multi-pronged approach. Sowing nuts in spring gives rodents less time to find and eat them, but traps, cats and serious control may also be needed. Netting the beds is fine protection against wind and birds, but I have yet to succeed in mouse-proofing a large seedbed. We used 1.6m-wide black 'shade' net stretched over hoops of old fencing wire pushed into the ground either side of the bed and held down with wire pegs. This is a simple, inexpensive system which can be erected over the seedbeds and left until the weeding becomes critical, then removed completely. It helps keep humidity high and bird predation at zero, but the mice, unfortunately, also enjoy the protection.

Irrigation

The most frequent cause of complete failure of a seedbed is probably drought following germination. It is hugely important to get an irrigation system established before sowing, as it can take an awful lot of watering-cans, used daily, to keep even a few square metres moist. The system will depend mainly on water supply, pressure and area. Special perforated hose is useful, particularly for smaller areas and low pressure, whereas a centrally controlled pumped sprinkler system is ideal, as long as the droplets are not so big that they can damage the seeds and seedlings.

Weeding

Tiny seedling trees cannot compete with vigorous weeds, so the only thing to do is tease out those unwanted plants to stop them smothering and, as important, to prevent them from seeding. I've been known to weed dock seedlings with tweezers from a bed of particularly rare Scots pine as it was the only way to remove the docks' excessively long root without disturbing the tiny pines. The whole nursery practice should be designed so as to minimise weed introduction, invasion or reproduction. Remember, 'one year's seeding, seven years' weeding'. Gradually the weed-seed bank will decline.

Emma Planterose Magenta

was one of the founders of Reforesting Scotland. With her then husband, Bernard, she ran a tree nursery in north-west Scotland and planted trees on Isle Martin. She now lives at Findhorn where she works and trains ponies and people in permaculture.

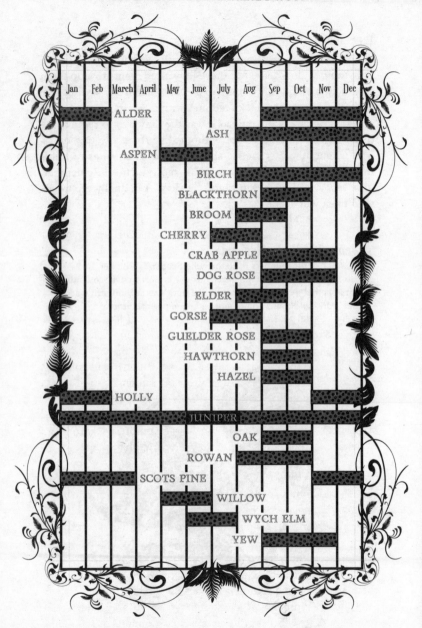

Seed calendar of Scotland's native species.

SEED
PROVENANCE
& THE LAW

Some things change with time and others don't; and one of the benefits of the passage of time is that you can look back with some satisfaction at things that have changed in positive ways. Which, for the most part, is what has happened with native woodlands. In the world of native seed collection, many millions of seeds have been collected and many millions of trees have been raised and planted. And whilst the regulations around seed collection have no doubt frustrated us all at times, the whole system has held together and allowed this impressive progress. So what exactly has stayed the same and what has changed ?

Starting with things that have stayed the same

It is still true that seed and plant regulations only apply when seeds or plants are marketed. So you can still collect seed and grow trees for your own use in any way you like; regulations do not apply here at all. However, if you pass your seeds on to a commercial nursery to grow on for you, that means they are effectively 'marketed' and the regulations will apply, even if all the plants are being returned to your ownership.

Consumer protection legislation applies to seed and plants to ensure that sellers provide accurate descriptions of seeds and plants, and only sell them when they are in good condition.

More importantly, we still have 'registered seed stands', which are seed sources chosen because of their high timber quality; and the process of regulating collection from these sources is still broadly the same. This includes informing the Forestry Commission prior to seed collection so that they can inspect your collection operation, and applying for a certificate that provides the basis of documentation which will accompany the seed and the plants raised from it through the marketing process.

The requirement to test seed for purity and germinability when seed is traded is still the same. The good intention of this provision, to assure the buyer of the quality of the seed, is as valid as ever; but so too are problems of the high costs this adds to small seed lots.

Nurseries are still inspected to ensure compliance with the provisions of the Forest Reproductive Materials regulations.

So what has changed?

One aspect is that the provisions are now too extensive to give an adequate description in a short article like this, as it arguably was in 1989! So the ambition in this current article is limited to providing a reasonable summary and to point readers in the direction of key documents and web pages. The main changes have resulted from two initiatives:

- Efforts by Forestry Commission and Forestry Research to develop a system to help regulate trade in locally sourced seed and stock of native species of trees and shrubs. This was in response to the expanding use of native species and recognised the fact that existing provisions developed for timber species – as highlighted in my original Reforesting Scotland article – were not always adequate.

- A shake-up of EU seed regulations that made its way into law via the Forest Reproductive Material (Great Britain) Regulations 2002 (FRMR), which regulate marketing of seed, cuttings and plants for 46 species and the genus *Populus* (see Forestry Commission 2007).

The new "local provenance" system developed by the Forestry Commission (see Herbert *et al*, 1999) centres on a map of native seed zones (see figure 1). This is used firstly to identify where seed and cuttings collections and potential planting sites are located (i.e., by using the local native seed zone number) and secondly as a basis for describing how far it is advisable to move seed and cuttings from their source to the planting site. The idea of this is to limit the movement of seed and cuttings by attempting to encourage use of seed from the same zone as the planting site; or if this is not possible, from neighbouring zones. The system also attempts to limit elevational transfers by applying 300m vertical elevation zones. Note, however, that this map does not apply to Scots pine, for which the original zones of biochemical similarity are used in a similar way.

Why were these changes made?

The main changes resulting from the revised Forest Reproductive Material Regulations were made in order to:

- extend regulation that had formerly only applied to oak, Scots pine and aspen to all Scottish native tree and shrub species;

- include a new category of seed source called 'source-identified', for which no timber quality criteria apply. This covers the types of seed source typically used for local provenance seed collection. Four main categories of source are now recognised: source-identified, selected (for registered seed stands) and qualified and tested (for seed from tree improvement programmes);

- provide traceability via an inspection and certification scheme to ensure that information about seed and cuttings collections passed with each lot from collection to planting out. The aim of this is to ensure that seed collected in, say, Caithness cannot be conveniently relabelled and sold as if it originated in Kirkudbright, Crathes or Kyle of Lochalsh;

- require suppliers of seed and cuttings to register with the Forestry Commission via a Register of Suppliers. Under the regulations, only registered suppliers can market seeds, cuttings and plants.

A seed supplier or nursery wishing to carry out local provenance seed collections now needs to follow a closely specified procedure. Firstly the supplier or nursery must be registered with the Forestry Commission. Then the seed source (even if source-identified) must be identified and prior notice given to the FCS of the intention to collect. After collection, a form (FRM4) must be obtained and filled out stating when and where the collection was made and the type and amount of seed collected. This is then submitted to the Forestry Commission (FC), who then issue a Master Certificate. When a supplier markets seed (or seedlings grown on from it), customers must be issued with a Supplier's Document containing information about the collection, including the number of the Master Certificate and the location where the seed was collected, although the latter does not have to be more specific than the native seed zone.

The net effect of these changes was to provide a regulatory system which brought all native seed collections and planting stock under a reasonable degree of control to help prevent abuse, such as collectors or nurseries selling lots which are deliberately or accidentally wrongly described. Another key advance was the inclusion of source-identified material, which got around some of the difficulties of the previous system for local tree nurseries growing EU species such as oak. The main downsides have been the increase in costs associated with inspections, certification, registration and seed testing. For small local tree nurseries, most of whom are rarely if ever tempted to wrongly describe seed or plants, there is a certain feeling that a large hammer has been used to crack a small nut. However, abuse does occur and needs to be minimised and it is in the interests of most seed collectors and nurseries to comply with the regulations. As such, the system has undoubtedly strengthened the sector as a whole.

The future

There is no doubt a case for reviewing the regulations now that they have been in force for a while to see whether there is scope to reduce the bureaucratic burden and/or tighten any loopholes if there is evidence of problems. Another priority is to make sure that the local provenance provisions of the native seed zones accurately reflect emerging scientific data on provenance variation, so as to ensure that the transfer rules (how far seed can be moved from source to planting site) are actually appropriate, especially if climate change manifests itself as predicted. Lastly, there needs to be some recognition that the transfer rules for seed and plants of native species produced from tree improvement programmes should allow greater flexibility (longer transfer distance) than for local provenance collections.

As for me, I spend far less time swinging around in the canopy of trees collecting seed than I did twenty years ago; but it was fun and I should make sure I carve out more time to do that again. After all, isn't fifty the new thirty – or something like that?

A final blinding change is that we can now all find information on the Internet. So try the following:

- http://www.forestry.gov.uk/forestry/INFD-66SG3X
- http://www.forestry.gov.uk/pdf/fcfc003.pdf/$FILE/ fcfc003.pdf

Dr Rick Worrell

Sources

Forestry Commission, *Regulations controlling seed, cuttings and planting stock for forestry in Great Britain*. Edinburgh, 2007.

Herbert, S. and Patterson, G., *Using local stock for planting native trees and shrubs*. Forestry Commission Information Note, Edinburgh, August 1999.

PART TWO

PROFILES OF
SPECIES IN
SCOTLAND

ALDER

Alnus glutosa / Fearn

The Gaelic for alder, *fearn*, is found in the place names of Glenfarne, Fearn, Ardfearn, Alltfearna, Glen Fearnach, and many others, showing the wide distribution of this tree in Scotland in earlier times. In Celtic mythology, alder is the tree of resurrection, marking the emergence of the solar year.

Where it grows

There is only one alder native to Britain and that is the common, or black, alder (*Alnus glutosa*). There are three other European alders, the grey alder (*A. incana*), the Italian alder (*A. cordata*) and the shrubby green alder, (*A. viridis*). Other alders you are likely to come across are Sitka alder (*A. sinuate*), and red, or Oregon, alder (*A. rubra*), the former being more a small tree or bush, from British Columbia and Alaska. All of them have been planted in Scotland, grey alder the most widely. It grows on drier sites than our native alder and on optimum sites, even faster. Red alder, the natural distribution of which practically coincides with Sitka spruce, has been trialled in Britain as a possible deciduous component in upland forestry, but it seems to be prone to frost. There may be more hope with a red/Sitka hybrid. Being essentially pioneer trees, all the alders are fast growing, Sitka and red being extremely fast. Even our common alder puts on 60–100cm of height growth a year in its first 15 to 20 years of life.

What to look for

The purple, twiggy outlines of alders stand out on riverbanks in winter, gaining depth in colour as the buds develop towards spring. The dark green, alternate, roundish leaves with toothed edges flush late in spring throughout Scotland. Both sexes of flower are borne on the same tree, the male catkins being long and purplish-brown, and the female ones small cylinders that develop into tiny cones.

As far as the tree-planting ecologist/forester is concerned, the most exciting thing about the whole family of alders is that they fix nitrogen. So alder can grow in very nitrogen-deficient soils and very wet conditions. In natural conditions it often forms a carr (a dense, swampy wood of lowish stature), or typically is found along watercourses of all sizes. It is specially adapted to dispersal by water, its seeds being flat and small with a margin of air-filled tissue. They will float for up to a month without becoming waterlogged. The cones themselves, being woody, will also float readily.

Cultivation

In the nursery, common alder presents no exceptional difficulties, though there are two important things to remember. One is that the seed should be watered practically every day that it does not rain, and this is also true for the newly geminated seedlings for the first 20 to 30 days. The second potential problem is that Mycorrhizal bacterium, *Frankia alni,* must be present in your nursery soil for the new seedlings to nodulate properly and therefore grow well. If it appears that you are not getting good nodulation – immediately recognisable by small yellow leaves and slow growth – dig up some root nodules from a mature tree, crush them up in water, and spray your seedbed with a watering can. If in doubt about the presence of *Frankia,* carry out this operation as part of preparing the seedbed.

Its nitrogen-fixing property confers on alders special significance for Scottish tree planters. The tree's nitrogen-rich leaves break down readily and improve soils for more various and demanding species to follow. We can use it to help reforest very poor sites where very few other deciduous trees can survive. It can grow on nutrient-poor upland sites; it is useful in derelict land reclamation, and it can be planted in very wet conditions where drainage might otherwise have seemed necessary to restore tree growth. It can tolerate a wide range of pH. In addition to all this, it is deep-rooting and very wind-firm and tolerant, although it is not very resistant to salt spray. In forester's terms, on good sites or poor, it will actually out-yield sycamore, birch and ash, giving a high-yielding crop on a short rotation. Although practically extinct in the far north-west and the Outer Isles, its natural distribution is thought to cover the entire country, so there are no worries, even when planting in these remote areas.

Collecting alder seed is easy, and you get a lot for a day's work. Pick the cones any time between the beginning of November and Christmas, avoiding the previous year's cones, which will be darker, more shrivelled, and obviously open. Dry them on trays in a warm room and then bash them about to release as much of the seed as possible. One method is to put them in a pillowcase and beat them with a rolling pin. Another is to place them in a bucket with a tightly fitting lid, and shake it vigorously. Sieve out the seed from the cones and store the seed in a cool, dry place until spring.

As with most light seeds, prepare a fine seedbed, broadcast the seed on the surface, and cover immediately with a very thin layer of fine grit. You should get about 40 seedlings for every 100g sown. Two-year-old transplants will be ready for planting out.

Uses

Historically, alder was highly prized as *the* charcoal wood for making gunpowder. Properly dried it makes excellent firewood, but when wet it will smoulder miserably. It is also traditionally the favourite wood of clog makers. It is certainly a good wood for turnery, being straight grained and therefore easy to cut. Its deep colour has even led it to be called 'Scotch mahogany'. Its water-resistance makes it good for walkways, waterwheels, piers, bridges and lock gates. Some alder wood ends up as handles for kitchen items and the backs of brushes. Small blocks used to be distributed around houses as a lure for woodworm, as the beetles favour the wood for laying their eggs. The trick was to burn them *before* the insects emerged. The leaves and bark can be used for making dyes. Alder coppices vigorously and therefore lends itself to wood production for these many specialist uses.

Lore

In Celtic legend, the alder is mentioned as a refuge, a dark hiding place. This may be for the good, as in the story of the eloping lovers Grainne and Diarmid, who hid from Finn MacCuil, or else it may be more sinister. Alder trees were reputed to be the hideaways of robbers and outlaws. Marion Campbell, the Argyll author and historian, suggested to Hugh Fife that some of the anxiety that surrounded the alder tree in Scottish minds may have been because of the way in which the cut timber turns blood red.

The Editorial Team

Sources

Donald MacVean's papers, published in *Ecology, 1955–59*, give a detailed account of the ecology of common alder. Forestry Commission *Bulletin 62* gives a silvicultural summary of the alder family in general, and some further references.

ASH
Fraxinus excelsior / Uinsinn

Uinsinn, the Gaelic for ash, is particularly common in Argyll place names such as Lan an uinsinn, Aird uinsinn, and Allt uinsinn. The Norse word for ash is *ask*, as in Port Askaig on Islay. It is a tree that comes into leaf late in the spring and loses its leaves early in autumn, yet grows faster than almost any other native hardwood.

Where it grows

Though the genus contains some 65 different species, there is just one that is native to Britain: the common ash (*Fraxinus excelsior*). American, Chinese and Caucasian ashes have all been planted as specimen trees, but the common ash is such a vigorous tree with such fine timber that there has been little incentive to seek a 'better' member of the genus. Common ash is distributed widely over most of Europe and southern Scandinavia. It reaches south to the shore of the Mediterranean (though it is absent from most of Spain) and east to the Caspian Sea, and is native to most of the counties of Scotland.

What to look for

The grey bark, knobbly twigs, and compound, pinnate leaves of ash should need no introduction. The flowers are less often noticed by the casual observer. Individual trees may bear wholly male, female or hermaphrodite flowers; alternatively, a mixture of both sexes occurs, with either dominating. Some trees even switch sex from year to year. In the spring, the dark flowers open from their distinctive black buds well before the leaves appear.

Growth of ash can be extremely rapid with height increments of 50–100cm in the first years. After about 45 years growth slows and it often stops at about 60 years. Top height can be between 20 and 30 metres, making it one of the three tallest trees native to Scotland. The root growth of the ash is prodigious, forcing its way through cracks in the bedrock to satiate its heavy demand for water. This feature of the tree explains its role in Norse mythology. It has a rich associated flora and fauna with 41 species of insect specifically adapted to it, and more than 225 epiphytic lichens have been recorded growing on it. Indeed, only oak has more. Ash is an important coppice tree and is usually cut on a 12- to 20-year rotation.

Where to plant it

Ash favours freely drained, moist, fertile soils of about neutral reaction (neither markedly acidic nor markedly alkaline) and will grow in many lowland and ex-agricultural sites. It is a demanding tree, having one of the highest nutrient-uptake requirements of any species. It is also relatively light-demanding, except as a seedling. In the Highlands it is harder to find suitable locations but it should be incorporated in mixed plantings except where the soil is acidic or inclined to wetness. In terms of climate, there is no reason why it should not be planted in the northern tip of the country, and it must once have been a major component in the forests of Sutherland where limestone outcrops. It is relatively salt-resistant but, though hardy and wind-firm, its 'thin' branching habit, late leafing, and early leaf-fall make it a relatively poor tree for shelterbelts.

Cultivation

Collect bunches of the winged seeds in late summer, when green, and sow immediately for moderate germination the following spring. Alternatively, collect when riper in the autumn and stratify in sand for two winters. In sheltered places the seed often stays on the tree all winter, so this is one species that you can get away with collecting late on the year. Towards the end of the second winter, sow thinly in rows or into a seedbed, and cover lightly with a mixture of soil and grit. Lime your bed if acidic and keep it from drying out, as with all germinating tree seed. Protect the beds from ice and birds with netting. There are about 1500 seeds per 100g. This weight of seeds spread over one square metre should yield about 375 seedlings. These will be ready for lining out after one or two years, giving planting stock after a further year. On good sites ash trees will produce seed every year. In less optimal sites, production may be cyclical. Dry ash seed retains high viability for up to seven years if kept in sealed polythene bags in a refrigerator at 2-4°C. Ash is very difficult to propagate vegetatively.

Uses

Ash is one of the very toughest of our native timbers, so it is utilised where there is need to absorb a hard blow or shock without splintering. It is used for tool handles, including those of hammers, axes, spades and pickaxes and for sports equipment such as hockey sticks, oars, and cricket stumps. It is widely used in furniture because of its strength and attractive grain, and also because it can easily be bent when steamed. Coppiced ash was traditionally made into charcoal. Ash leaves are still fed to cattle in Scandinavia, and the bark used for tanning nets. The ash is considered the queen of firewoods and burns well even when green.

Lore

In Norse mythology the ash is Yggdrasil, 'The World Tree' or 'Tree of Life', holding in its roots the whole world, and in its upper branches, the mansions of the gods. The three sisters of Fate, the past, present and future, are believed to have sprinkled the tree with pure water. An eagle, a squirrel, and a hawk lived in the branches and a serpent in the roots; a goat, which fed on the leaves, gave milk to the heroes of Valhalla, the Nordic heaven. Under the tree stood a horn, which would one day blow to announce the end of the universe.

The Editorial Team

ASPEN
Populus tremula / Crithen

The Latin name for European poplar is *Populus tremula,* tree of the people, whose ever-stirring leaves are like the ever-restless multitude of humankind, quickened into action by the slightest breath. The constantly moving foliage echoes the unceasing course of time itself.

Where it grows

The aspen is probably the only poplar native to Scotland, although both grey poplar (*Populus canescens*) and black poplar (*P. nigra*) can be found. Like other species in the poplar family, including hybrids, they are commonly planted. The distribution of European poplar extends through most of Europe, across Asia to Japan, as well as North Africa. In this country it ranges from the south-west tip of England to Shetland and the Western Isles. It stands to reason that its form will vary across such a wide range and locally adapted genotypes can be expected. In Scotland it is more common in the Highlands, especially in central Grampian and the west.

What to look for

Unlike the continental poplars we associate so readily with northern France, European aspen does not grow into a very tall tree, seldom exceeding 20 metres, and more usually about 10 metres tall in Scotland. Nonetheless, it typically has a straight stem, sparse branching, which contributes to a lean appearance, and pale bark which attracts attention in a winter landscape.

The leaves are oval to round with irregularly indented margins which, borne on long flattened stalks, catch the slightest breeze to tremble and rustle against each other. In autumn they can assume a beautiful bright yellow, such colouring being much more pronounced in the colder and drier interior of Scotland than it is on the west.

Aspen flowers in early spring before bud break, but in parts of north and west Scotland, it seems to set seed only very rarely. This is because most remaining groups of aspen are single clones, and so of just one sex. Few such groups are close enough to other clones for transmission of pollen for fertilisation. If this does occur, the catkins ripen in early summer, their seedpods splitting to release tiny seeds, tufted with hairs. But in Scotland the aspen spreads primarily by profuse suckering. It grows quickly but is short-lived, often surviving as little as 50 years.

Cultivation

In England aspen is mostly found in marshy spots on clay and other poor, moist soils. In Scotland it is often found clinging to the most exposed cliffs in the west, right by the sea. In the central Highlands, as in Scandinavia, it is most characteristically found in small pure stands on gravelly slopes or screes. It prefers neutral to acidic conditions and will not tolerate very dry soils or too much shade.

Aspen should be included particularly in upland plantings where a native type of woodland is being created or regenerated. As it will not form understorey, it should not be intimately mixed with trees that are likely to out-top it. Its natural companions will be birch, rowan and hazel; in a pinewood planting it can be added in groups on the shallower soils or at the wood margins where an area of bog, rock, or scree is left open.

On account of the fact that seed is not often found in Scotland and is difficult to handle and germinate in nursery conditions, we have to rely on vegetative propagation to perpetuate Scottish genotypes – and this, too, is not easy. As most of the aspen planted in Scotland in the twentieth century was of non-native stock, it is important to find genuinely wild trees from which to take cuttings. Unfortunately, hardwood cuttings have a poor success rate, so most trees are raised from root cuttings.

Roots of 1–3cm diameter can be taken from the parent tree in early March. Wash them, then cut to fit propagator trays, discarding pieces with badly damaged skins. Pack in the trays in a damp 50/50 mixture of perlite and compost or leaf mould and turn on the propagator. After two to three weeks shoots appear, and when they are 4–10cm long, cut them off with a very sharp knife. Plant these cuttings in a 50/50 mixture of perlite and vermiculite in another heated propagator, and they will start to root after one to three weeks. The rooted cuttings can then be planted in compost in pots and grown on. Meanwhile, new shoots grow from the original roots wherever cuttings have been taken, and these are cut in their turn and treated in the same way. Shoots continue to appear until the end of July or even mid-August.

If you do obtain seed from a more southerly parent tree, it is only viable for a few days once it is ripe. It germinates in just six days. The seed is difficult to work with because it is so tiny: there are around 1 million seeds per 100g. It requires a very fine seedbed and fine spray watering.

Aspen is one of only three native tree species in Scotland (oak and Scots pine being the other two) that are controlled by European regulations, and trees for sale for forestry purposes must be grown from registered sources.

Uses

Aspen wood is the best of all for making matches and is used for this purpose in Scandinavia, Poland and Russia. It is not planted for timber in the British Isles, but imported timber used to find its way into the manufacture of fruit boxes and baskets as well as matches. In the United States, as elsewhere, aspen has long been shunned as a finished timber but, more recently, it has increasingly been looked at as an alternative to pine, particularly for doors and window frames. Its light weight and colour would appear to make it perfectly suitable for these purposes, so long as it has had the correct processing. It is also becoming increasingly important for making OSB (oriented strand board) and for pulp production, on account of its ability to grow quickly and regenerate naturally from suckers.

In England, aspen was historically used for clogs and for arrow shafts, but in Scotland, because of its mythological associations, a taboo on the use of the wood for fishing and farming prevailed. With the upsurge of interest in our native hardwoods there is now hope that aspen will become a valued timber in this country and therefore will be included in enlightened forestry schemes.

Lore

By one Christian tradition it is a tree of mourning and sin because (according to this tradition) the cross of Christ's crucifixion was made of it, and so it trembles at the shame and horror of its past. To the Highland seer, its rustling sounds induced prophetic insight. Denoting good or evil, quite rarely or unexpectedly encountered, the aspen has always been something of an omen tree. The Gaelic name is Crithen, and is hard to find in place names; Blarcreen in Argyll, is an example.

The Editorial Team with notes from Michael Matthews

BEECH
Fagus sylvatica

Beech is not a native to Scotland, being a late colonist to southern England, and hence it features in Anglo-Saxon rather than Celtic lore. Yet it is now very much a feature of Scottish broadleaved woodlands, and in some areas its tall grey stems and huge domed crowns dominate the landscape, particularly along hedgerows. It thrives on suitable sites and regenerates freely. We can now only hypothesise as to what its natural range and dominance might have been without human intervention.

Where it grows

Beech belongs to the family *Fagaceae*, which includes oaks and sweet chestnuts, together with the southern hemisphere beeches. The genus *Fagus* has ten species, all occurring in northern temperate regions. *Fagus sylvatica L.* the common, or European, beech is the only one of these that is native to the British Isles. Its natural distribution in southern England is only as far west as Dorset, to East Anglia, and north to the Midlands, possibly including part of South Wales. It is found naturally throughout Europe as far east as Bulgaria and north to parts of Norway and Sweden.

Palaeological studies have shown that beech was slow to colonise Britain after the last ice age but that in historic times its rate of expansion has not decreased. This suggests a species that had not reached its climatic limit in Britain, which is consistent with observations on its performance over most of its natural range.

This supports the conservation of mature beech trees where they occur in Scotland. The biodiversity value which ‹near-neighbour› trees such as beech offer to Scottish woodlands is as much to do with their age as their species, and their cultural value may also be highly significant. If, however, you were planting a strictly ‹new native› woodland, beech could not be part of it, as all trees would have to be local genotypes conforming to the National Vegetation Classification (NVC).

What to look for

Beech is a shade-tolerant tree that does not readily colonise new sites – it is not a pioneer species. Slow-growing at first, on good sites it can reach a height of 40m in 120 years. Budburst is in late April to May, the leaves being covered in silky white hairs, which are lost as the leaf expands. The leaf is glossy, dark green above and paler below. Foliage can look dark, olive green from a distance in mid-summer. Leaf fall is in November, younger plants and hedges tending to retain the brown leaves throughout the winter. Bark is usually smooth grey and unfissured; winter buds are brown and elongated with sharp tips.

Beech responds well to clipping and hence is popular as a hedge species. The 30m-high hedge at Meikelour, in Perthshire, is a notable, if extraordinary, example. It does not respond well to surgery however, taking a long time to recover from the removal of large branches. It also coppices very poorly. It can be a very long-lived tree and the oldest individuals, up to 1000 years old, form some of Britain's largest broadleaves. Copper and purple-leaved forms are often planted in policy woodlands.

Where to plant

Beech will do well on a variety of sites but, in planting, avoid extremes of pH, peaty, shallow, or waterlogged soils. It grows best of all on deep, well-drained loams of moderate alkalinity. It is naturally associated with chalky soils but almost any light, free-draining soil will do.

It is surprisingly tolerant of exposure but can be difficult to establish on a bare site, owing to its susceptibility to spring frosts. Generally beech grows better with side-shelter or light overhead cover for the first few years, making it a useful species for underplanting or restocking old woodlands. However, it has a tendency to shade out other tree species and most ground vegetation. It should not be used to underplant native oakwoods as it would eventually take them over.

Cultivation

Heaviest crops of seed are produced by trees between 80 and 100 years old. Mast years occur at infrequent intervals, of five to 15 years in Britain, usually following warm, dry summers. Seed can be collected by gathering from the base of selected trees between September and November, there being about 400 seeds per 100g. Viability can be expected at around 60 per cent. Although there are 15 registered seed stands in Britain, it should be noted that beech seed has been imported for at least 200 years, and most existing stands are probably not of native origin.

Seed should be sown immediately in nursery rows, protected from mice, and left undisturbed for the first year. Thinning to 10cm intervals can take place when the first true leaf shows, and then plants should be lined out at 30cm intervals for one or two years.

In Europe, beech was traditionally planted densely (0.33 x 1.00m) to suppress side branching and produce upright trees. It does, however, respond well to planting in tree shelters, which accelerate early growth and perhaps can protect from early frost. However, there is a suggestion that 1.2m high shelters may promote fungal infections in young plants. Drilled, or netting, shelters are now available to assist air-flow and reduce this problem. Grey squirrels have been notorious for damaging beech trees by eating bark, particularly in woods where density is high, and the trees range from 15 to 40 years old.

Uses

Beech is potentially one of the most valuable home-grown hardwoods. The wood is generally pale brown in colour, and marked with many small, dark flecks. It is hard and strong and can be worked in any direction. The highest quality timber has a whiteness and absence of defects, and is in demand for furniture and veneers.

Beech is also used to make small objects such as bowls, spoons, mallet heads, tool handles, and parts of pianos. The roundwood makes good charcoal, may be used for turnery, and can also go for pulp.

Historically, chips of beech wood were used to clarify wine. The earliest runes were written on beech board: the Anglo-Saxon word *bece* means both 'beech' and 'book'. Leaves were once collected in the autumn, before the first frost, and used to stuff mattresses. Boiled leaves were used by herbalists, both as poultices and in ointments. Although the tree bears nuts irregularly, some can usually be found every three to five years. In some parts of Europe they are pressed to release their oil for 'beech butter'. In France they are roasted to make a kind of coffee.

Keith Logie
is a Chartered Forester who has spent many years dealing with elms and Dutch Elm disease. He works for the City of Edinburgh Council managing greenspace strategy and specialist services.

Thorunn Helgason
is an Ecology Lecturer at the University of York. Her research focusses on the biodiversity of mycorrhizal fungi.

BIRCH
Betula

Birch is the tree that represents the second letter of the Gaelic tree alphabet, *beith*, as used in Cowdenbeath in Fife, and Beith in Ayrshire. It is handmaiden to the queen, 'Critheann', or aspen – the third letter of the tree alphabet, which all children in the Highlands once learnt by heart, whilst acquiring a knowledge of the natural environment.

The different Scottish species

Four birches exist in Scotland, but the debate on their taxonomy suffers more from heat than light in respect to the status as full species of at least one of them.

The best known of all species, the silver birch (*Betula pendulata syn. B. verrucosa*) is the tallest and most productive species of all birches including the North American species. Silver birch is a tree of the drier mineral soils and, typically for a pioneer tree, it is a marvellous soil improver. Confusingly, not all trees of this species are pendulous and, of those that are, some are more so than others. Indeed, many trees are decidedly not pendulous at all, which often leads to confusion with other species. Silver birch can attain height of between 15 and 25 metres, and occasionally more.

A good guide to identification is that, at all ages, silver birch has little white markings on its twigs (lenticels), which are not found on downy birch. But beware, because, when very young and usually in only the first four years of growth, leaves can be fairly pubescent (hairy), which does lead to confusion in nurseries. The leaves of silver birch are remarkably toothed, regardless of age, and of a lighter green than other native birches. In the autumn they turn a beautiful golden yellow.

Downy birch (*Betula pubescens*) is the next species that most people are familiar with. It is common in lowland areas on wetter sites, often with higher humus content, which it can tolerate quite well. Not as fast-growing as silver birch, but quite fast nevertheless, this tree is also a soil improver. It can often be found growing amongst silver birch as well as in pure stands or mixed with willows. Downy birch can grow to height of between 15 and 20 metres.

The leaves and twigs of downy birch are downy to the touch, and the leaves are more rounded in shape, with less pronounced toothed edges, than silver birch. The leaf colour is a rather duller olive hue compared with that of silver birch and, when frosted, turns to a darker shade of gold.

The third species, or subspecies, is mountain birch (*Betula tortuosa [Ledeb.] syn. B. pub. odorata, or B. pub. carpatica*). Both are found in central and southern Europe, the original descriptions of which do not match up with the trees we have growing in northern Scotland.

Without going into too much detail, mountain birch is apolycormic with very poor apical dominance. In other words, it is multi-stemmed and of very poor form from the timber production point of view. Nothing is known of its yield in conventional terms, but, at a guess, I would imagine that it is unlikely to exceed General Yield Class 4, as it reaches only a height of 5 to 15 metres.

This birch is found on a variety of soils under poor climatic conditions including high exposure. In the central Highlands, it begins to appear at an altitude of about 250m, but in the northwest it can be found at, or close to, sea level.

One interesting feature of this tree is that it freely intergrades with dwarf birch *Betula nana* throughout northern Europe. However, due to the decimation of our dwarf birch population, this can only rarely happen in Scotland. The population at Glen Loyal is an example that may represent the largest remnant of this genetic 'swarm' between what may be the two evolutionary extremes of a possible 'superspecies'.

Mountain birch has the interesting characteristic of releasing chemicals from its leaves which inhibit the needle growth of conifers. For this reason, in parts of Sweden it is known as 'perpetual birch', as the normal successional growth from birch to spruce/pine fails to take place. This phenomenon seems to be the adaptation of a slow and low-growing tree which prevents it, a light-demander like all birches, from being shaded out by faster (and ultimately taller) conifers. I have actually seen the effect that mountain birch had in inhibiting the growth of Douglas fir that had been underplanted in a wood in Inverness-shire.

The last of our birches is the dwarf birch (*Betula nana*), more a plant, for it never is a tree in the usual sense of the word. Little is known or understood about dwarf birch in Scotland, particularly its distribution. The plant often appears within fenced-off areas, wherever burning or severe grazing pressure has been removed. This suggests that the distribution is much wider than thought, as dwarf birch reproduces itself very effectively vegetatively as well as by seed throughout its worldwide distribution.

It seems fairly certain that the root systems continue to exist despite centuries of being eaten back. We do know that all birches maintain dormant buds, both below and above ground, throughout their entire lives, and that this can be for several rotations – in effect, natural coppicing.

What to look for

Whilst birch is a colonist and capable of growth under extreme conditions, as timber and as a soil improver it is most productive on mineral soils. Within only a decade or two it can take a podsoil site and convert it to a brown earth with an ever-increasing pH. The rate at which nutrient cycling takes place is pretty spectacular due to the production of 3 to 4 tonnes of leaf litter per hectare per annum.

The initial growth curve for birch is much faster than for any other north European species, except possibly alder. The optimum rotation for birch would seem to be about 40 years, after which growth rates drop off and are overtaken by pine and spruce.

Birches of all species are strong light-demanders. When grown under spacing conditions either of natural regeneration or plantation (at no less than 2500 per hectare), a natural pruning takes place with small-diameter branches dying and being knocked off during thinning or by the weight of wet snow.

One of the features of birch is its natural deep rooting: you rarely see a wind-blown birch! When grown in an intimate mixture with conifers, particularly spruces, this can have a marked improvement on stand stability – something that could be of wide future benefit to commercial forestry in Scotland. This is a sobering thought when one considers the amounts of money squandered in the past by the expensive removal (weeding!) of natural regeneration of birch from spruce and pine plantings.

Another feature noted in Scandinavia has been the reduction in the incidence of butt rot in spruce when grown in a mixture with birch. The reason appears to be due to the strain of butt rot in spruce and birch being different, the birch effectively functioning as a barrier between infected and healthy spruce root systems.

Finally, this symbiosis between birch and pine/spruce has already been demonstrated to increase yield per hectare as well as to give a beneficial increase in log quality.

Cultivation

A prolific seed producer, sadly, more seed is produced by trees of poor form than by those with desirable characteristics and, as there is a high level of inheritability form birch, it is very important to collect from the very best trees.

Ripe catkins can be collected from July onwards, preferably well before the catkins begin to crumble. They can still be quite green and firm when gathered. Spread the catkins out in trays or fish boxes to dry naturally in a warm room or shed. They must be properly dried before bagging if they are to be stored over winter. The bags then need to be put in the fridge at 2–4°C for the winter.

The seed is most often broadcast sown in the spring (although it can be autumn sown) on to a fine seedbed and covered with a very thin layer of grit. The secret is to water the seedbeds frequently, probably every day that it does not rain. When germination begins, keep watering, a little but frequently. Most wholesale failures of birch in a nursery are due to drying out.

One kilo of birch seed contains about 2 million seeds and should produce about 100,000 seedlings. Broadcast seed at between 5 and 15 grammes per square metre, depending on viability (in turn dependent on seed source, storage conditions, age of seed etc).

Bare roots of birch, if exposed to the wind, are killed off in as short a space of time as 20 minutes. This explains one of the complaints about birch that it is 'difficult to establish'. What is needed is either skilful handling or the use of cell-grown stock. I have found mortality to stand at less than 5 per cent with cell-grown birch, with early establishment, providing weed competition (particularly from bracken) is low in the first few years.

Where to plant it

Whilst birch is a wonderful tree, it is not a 'wonder tree'. The first consideration when planting it is to use local, or as near local as possible, provenance seed. The second is to opt for silver birch if possible, and that means a fairly dry site with very thin peat, if any.

The yield of silver birch is some 20 per cent better than downy birch. However, whilst downy birch will be quite happy on dry sites, silver birch will *not* be able to grow satisfactorily on wet sites or those with high humus content or deep peat. In fact, downy birch on peaty sites deeper than 1.0m is not to be advised either.

The only reason for planting mountain birch would be as part of an ecological restoration project. From a timber production point of view, there do not seem to be any areas at this time, even at high elevations, which could profitably grow this species.

Uses

The timber of both silver birch and downy birch has been tested beside other timbers by the Timber Research and Development Association and found to be the equal of beech, ash and sycamore in terms of nailing, gluing, bending and tensile strength. It will dry rapidly enough by air or kiln and is very stable, though unsuitable for outdoor uses unless treated.

Current uses include furniture, flooring, wall panelling, plywood, barrel manufacture, toys, and food utensils.

There is a range of wood grain types found in birch, all largely 'white wood' but either plain, flecked, or wavy. There are also the very rare and attractive flamed, curly and burred grains, which are expensive and much sought after.

Hornbeam

A fine member of the birch family that is not native to Scotland, and is only seen in parks, gardens and estates in the south of the country, is the hornbeam (*Carpinus betulus*). In general form it resembles the beech, but its catkins give away its actual family allegiance. Hornbeams are tolerant of pruning and partial shade, so in warm situations at altitudes of up to 500m they can be used for hedging. The wood is extremely hard and strong – the tree is also known as 'ironbeam' – and has been used for everything from machine cogs to chopping blocks and golf club heads, as well as making excellent firewood and good charcoal.

Iain Brodie

formerly ran the Birch Improvement Company in the Highlands, carrying out extensive provenance and fertilisation trials with silver and downy birch. In 1994 he started The Auchgourish Botanic Garden near Boat of Garten. He now has extensive plant collections from the northern hemisphere and a plant nursery with a shop.

Sources

There is very little available in English on the silviculture of birch. However, much of the above has been adapted from *Management guidelines for birch in the uplands* by the author.

Forestry Commission, *Birch in the uplands:*
www.forestry.gov.uk/pdf/UplandBirchwoods.pdf/$FILE/
    UplandBirchwoods.pdf

Hornbeam paragraph added by the editors.

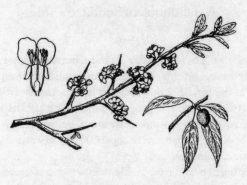

BLACKTHORN
Prunus spinosa / Draoighinn

Familiar to most for its fruit, the sloe, this tree gets its name from its black, thorny twigs, which are particularly noticeable when the tree is in flower. The Gaelic name is *Draoighinn* and it occurs in such place names as Port na Drioghearn on Islay, Ardindrean in Wester Ross, and Auchindrain in Argyll. Although in Gaelic folklore it has dark and negative connotations, it also symbolises protection and security, and this duality is perhaps illustrated by an old saying translated from Gaelic, 'Better the bramble than the blackthorn, but better the blackthorn than the devil'.

Where it grows

Blackthorn, or sloe, *Prunus spinosa* is native throughout Europe and into Asia. In Britain it is found in every county from Sutherland southwards, up to an altitude of 400 metres, although it is absent from some of the Northern Isles. It occurs on open ground and in scrub, woods and hedges on a great variety of soils. Its small flowers, which open well before the leaves, and early flowering time (March–April) help to distinguish it from the other common plum species, Wild Plum, *Prunus domestica*, and its subspecies, the Bullace, *P.institua*, both of which tend to flower later.

What to look for

Blackthorn is a bush or small tree growing to 4m and frequently suckering to form dense thickets. The specific name *spinosa* conveys one of the most characteristic features of the plant, namely its spiny habit. Thorns appear on the parent branches, thickening at the base, and then growing into small branches, still with a thorn at the tip. At about 15cm in length, the thorn dies away and the twig becomes a proper branch. The thorns are a frequent cause of deep wounds in animals, being able to penetrate a cow's hoof and cause severe sepsis. They can also inflict damage on bicycle and even car tyres!

Blackthorn bears fruit in September and October: drupes with a shiny skin and attractive blue bloom. But the species is most famous as a hedge plant, with its bushy, branching habit and vicious spines. Its impenetrable nature provides excellent nesting cover for birds. It is also the food plant of the larvae of brown and black hairstreak butterflies, although these do not occur in Scotland. Few birds will eat large quantities of the sloes, but some, in particular finches, will eat a lot if they sense the approach of a hard winter. Small rodents will also take the fruits.

Where to plant

The blackthorn has been much neglected in modern times and is generally regarded as an unwanted and invasive scrub species. The main reason for planting it now is as a hedging plant but, as a thicket, it also provides an invaluable shelter for wildlife and game. As a plant it is completely hardy, but the flowers can be damaged by severe late frosts – hence the expression 'blackthorn winter', which refers to a cold snap in the early spring. It is not tolerant of heavy shade but stands exposure to wind and can provide good shelter along the woodland edge. Its tolerance of salt spray makes it ideal for planting on coastal sites.

It can be planted on a wide variety of soil types, being tolerant of very dry and nutrient-poor sites, although very wet sites should be avoided. It grows vigorously and responds well to cutting and browsing.

Cultivation

Propagation is best done from seed. Gather the fruits as soon as they ripen and stratify in coarse sand for two winters, protecting them well from mice. Alternatively, allow the fruit to rot in a plastic bag, remove the flesh, and stratify the seed for one winter only. Sow in nursery rows in late winter or early spring and a few plants may be big enough (30cm or greater) to plant by the first autumn. If you leave the bed for a second year, more seeds may germinate. Suckers and root cuttings provide alternative methods of propagation.

Uses

Blackthorn is the ancestor of our cultivated plum, and man has been eating its fruits for thousands of years. Its domestication first gave us the damson and then, crossed with the cherry plum of western Asia, resulted in the large sweet plums of our gardens and orchards.

The sloe makes such a good wine that 200 years ago it was used by fraudulent wine merchants for adulterating port wine. In Ireland the leaves were made into a rather astringent tea. Nowadays the astringency is tempered by using the fruits for jam and jelly, sometimes with apple, and also as a fine flavouring in sloe gin.

The thorns are so tough that they were once used as sewing needles. The twigs were used by early water diviners. The bark was used medicinally and for tanning leather. The wood is valued for walking sticks because of its lightness, strength and pliability. The spiralling quality of honeysuckle and other climbers growing on blackthorn gives the crooked form to the traditional Highland stick. The wood is also used in marquetry, as it has fine, dark markings on a light matrix.

Lore

The blackthorn is symbolic of austerity, difficulty and ill luck, once even regarded as an omen of death, and according to Christian legend Christ's crown of thorns was woven from its branches. Witches were believed to carry blackthorn rods, and these were often burnt with them.

Martin Howard
is an ecologist, a founder, and a former Director of Reforesting Scotland.

BUSHES

Blaeberry

Blaeberry, *Vaccinium myrtillus*, is a small deciduous shrub that is commonly known as bilberry south of the Border. It is found on acid soils, growing both on open moorland, where it reaches a height of 1.25m, and as a ground layer in light canopied woodland. It is a common plant in Scotland, particularly in the north and west. It can tolerate very dry conditions and extremely acidic peat and often grows with cowberry, *V. vitis-idaea*. It is very tolerant of exposure but also withstands shade and is thus able to grow in places where heather fails to become established. On open moorland, however, heather is usually the dominant shrub, with blaeberry surviving in its shade but rarely flowering. The fruits are blue-black in colour when ripe and are of great value to birds, providing an important part of the diet of moorland birds such as ptarmigan, grouse, partridge, and pheasant. They are also eaten by mistle and song thrushes, and the plants themselves provide food for a number of insects. Blaeberry is generally pollinated by bees and wasps but can be self-pollinating.

Propagation can be carried out by a variety of methods, although the easiest is by cuttings. Propagation by seed is also possible, but germination can be erratic and slow.

The fruits are greatly valued by humans, and although they are time-consuming to pick and difficult to store, the delicate taste makes it worth the effort. The use of berry scoops makes picking easier. The long association with this useful plant has led to a large number of different names around the country. The name bilberry derives from the Danish *bollebar*, meaning 'dark berry' and the Scots blaeberry from the old Norse *blaa*, meaning 'blue'. The southern name, whortleberry, may be a corruption of myrtleberry. The plant is also called whinberry and huckleberry, and the fruit 'hurt' or 'whort'.

The Ancient Britons used blaeberry juice to stain their faces, and later it was used as a blue dye for linen and paper. The fruit is excellent eaten raw but is also used for pies, jellies and jams. It is rich in Vitamin C. Herbalists have used the juice in the form of syrup to treat lung diseases, vomiting, and stomach upsets. In Scotland, the leaves were once used for tea.

The bog bilberry, *V. uliginosum*, is a more northern species, also found in Scotland. Both the berries and leaves have a stronger blue colour.

Bog Myrtle

Bog Myrtle, *Myrica gale*, also known as sweet gale, is a small deciduous shrub, growing to 1–2m in height, and containing many resin glands which give it a strong, aromatic fragrance. It is a plant of wet ground, usually found on bogs and acid heaths, although it can tolerate neutral soils and was common in the fen country of East Anglia before it was drained. Its roots develop nitrogen-fixing nodules which enable it to get its nitrogen from the air rather than the ground. This allows it to thrive where there is a permanently high water table. It is widespread in Britain, particularly on the west, reaching an altitude of 550 metres. Dispersal is by small, sticky seeds which are produced in August and September. Propagation is easiest by layering but it is also possible from seed, treating it like birch seed, and keeping seeds and young plants well watered.

The main value of bog myrtle lies in the leaves, which were used for flavouring ale long before hops were brought into Britain. In Sweden it was forbidden to gather the blossoms before a certain date in the year, in order to conserve the plant. Isolated patches around old monasteries may date back to Anglo-Saxon times, when they were probably cultivated for this purpose.

In many places the fruits were dried and used as a spice for flavouring soups and stews, and sprigs for flavouring spirits. Combined with water, honey and lemon juice, a well-flavoured gale mead can be produced. In Scotland the aromatic branches are used to repel midges, and the leaves to scent linen and keep moths away. There are now commercial midge repellents made from bog myrtle.

Bramble

The bramble, *Rubus fruticosus*, must be one of the most familiar plants to most of us, with memories of childhood berry-picking and its associated scratches. Beatrix Potter immortalised these in *Peter Rabbit*, the story of a bunny who had frequent tangles with brambles. In Christian tradition the bramble is an emblem of Christ and the Virgin Mary, and in folklore an arch of bramble was said to be an effective cure for man or horse.

Bramble occurs throughout Europe, being found in wood-land, especially on drier soils where it forms dense masses. It is also common in hedgerows. However, it fruits and flowers more freely in open situations. There are nearly three hundred recognised taxa (species and varieties), some of them producing bigger and more palatable fruits than others, although birds and mammals are probably less discriminating about their different merits than are people. Bramble flowers appear from May to September and attract butterflies and other insects to their ample supplies of sweet-scented nectar. The fruits ripen from late July but are said to have no value after the start of November, when they may have been 'spat on', or worse, by the devil. They certainly lose their flavour after the first real frosts.

Tip-layering is the easiest method of propagation, being the plant's natural method of spreading, but plants can also be raised from seed. The bramble is able to reproduce apomectically, that is, it can set seed without being fertilised, but occasionally cross-pollination occurs, leading to hybridisation.

The succulent fruits have been in use by humans for thousands of years; bramble seeds were found in the stomach of a Neolithic man in Essex. They make excellent pies and jam and can be bottled or frozen. The juice of the fruits yields a dye that is grey on wool and slate blue on silk, whilst the green shoots produce a black dye. Although we have lost many brambles with the decline of hedgerows, this plant is a survivor and readily appears on any neglected land.

Broom

Broom, *Cytisius scoparius*, is a deciduous shrub with erect, wiry branches and rich, bright-yellow flowers. The seeds are borne in black-brown, hairy, flattened pods, which open explosively to aid dispersion. It is typical of light, sandy and acidic soils, particularly in scrub and heathland communities and on waste ground. The plant can spread rapidly into clear-fell sites, producing dense thickets 2–5m high. This invasive characteristic can cause problems on some sites. However, its nitrogen-fixing abilities make it a valuable plant for infertile ground, such as in land-reclamation schemes. It occurs on the edge of woods but is very light-demanding and does not stand heavy shade.

There are many insects associated with broom, and it provides food for the larva of the green hairstreak butterfly. The seedpods are attractive to ants.

Broom is easy to propagate from seed, with the pods opening naturally if stored in a warm, dry place. The seeds should be soaked in just-boiled water for up to 24 hours before sowing. The seedlings grow quickly in the nursery and should be planted before they grow too much, as larger plants transplant less well. Often, direct seeding can be the best way of establishing the plant.

Buckthorn

There are several species of buckthorn in Britain but only sea buckthorn, *Hippophae rhamnoides*, has naturally found its way into Scotland. Alder buckthorn, *Frangula alnus*, and purging buckthorn, *Rhamnus cathaticus*, occur south of the Border. Buckthorn is the Christian symbol of martyrdom and some sources claim that Christ's crown of thorns was made of buckthorn. In ancient

Greece buckthorn was believed to have the power to ward off evil spirits, and it was much used in England in the Middle Ages to protect against the effects of witchcraft. The berries of the purging buckthorn are a powerful cathartic, but the severity of their action has eventually led to their being considered unsafe.

The sea buckthorn is a deciduous, suckering shrub, usually growing up to 3m tall, but it can achieve 9m and become tree-like in certain situations. The leaves are long and narrow, turning from a silvery green colour to a dull grey-green with maturity. The berry-like orange fruits are borne in great profusion and contain a single hard black seed.

The plant is very hardy and drought-resistant, growing chiefly on stable coastal sand dunes but also on soft cliffs. In Scotland its main distribution is along the East Coast. The chief limiting factor to its growth is its demand for light – mature plants being quickly shaded out if trees invade the stand. It is able to colonise sand dunes due to its ability to produce abundant suckers. Its nitrogen-fixing nodules enable it to cope with very infertile soils.

Production of its bright orange fruits is usually prolific, and germination is high where both sexes are present in a stand. The most usual method of propagation is from seed, although vegetative methods are also possible. However, stratification for 18 months is necessary to break dormancy, with a temperature of below 5°C.

Sea buckthorn has a valuable role in sand-dune stabilisation, but care should be taken to avoid planting it near other established natural dune vegetation, as it is likely to be invasive. The fruits provide important food for some birds, particularly migrating fieldfares, starlings and waxwings, on their arrival in autumn.

The fruits are not generally used by humans in Britain, although there is a growing interest in them for preparing fruit cordials because of their high Vitamin C content. They are greatly valued in Russia. There, buckthorn is widely planted, often in conjunction with Norway spruce, and specialist seed orchards exist for this purpose. Collecting the fruits, which are used for preserves and for medicinal purposes, is a national pastime, rivalling mushroom and pine nut foraging. Vendors can often be seen at the roadside.

Gorse

Gorse is held to be under the domain of Mars, partly due to its yellow flowers, and partly to its inhospitable spines. Many people have marvelled at its beauty, including the botanists Dillenius and Linnaeus, who is said to have got down on his knees when he was shown a gorse-covered common in London, and thanked God 'for its loveliness'. He later spent years trying unsuccessfully to introduce gorse to Sweden.

Gorse (*Ulex europaeus*) is a member of the *leguminosae* family, and is one of the plants that has nearly as many colloquial names as the Guelder Rose. They include furze, vuzz, whine, hawth, goss and goose (in much of the north of England) but in Scotland it is usually known as whin. The Latin *Ulex* is thought to have come from the Celtic '*ec*' or '*oc*', meaning prickle or sharp point. Anyone who has tried to cross a gorse-covered common will see that this appropriate.

Gorse can be found right across the UK, growing on acid, sandy, heathland soils, often in highly exposed situations. It is thought not to be indigenous to Scotland, as it often flowers during the winter. The romantic saying 'When gorse is out of bloom, kissing's out of season' and the patriotic one, 'While gorse is in flower, Britain shall never be conquered' both illustrate the range of months in which the yellow flowers can be found.

Broom, (*Cystus scoparius*) is similar, though unrelated to gorse, having no spines and only flowering in May and June. Confusingly, it can also be referred to as whin.

Gorse is a dense woody shrub, up to 2m high, with very dark green foliage and spines formed from matured leaves. The majority of plants will flower in spring and summer, though flowers can be found at all times (see above). Seeds are produced in long, thin pods that burst open during dry summer months to spread the seed. The denser, double varieties, together with two dwarf varieties (*U. minor and U.nanus*) are usually preferred for garden planting and produce an effective burglar-proof hedge. During dry weather, gorse can burn ferociously, with catastrophic consequences on large gorse heaths, although it will quickly regenerate from seed.

Gorse likes acid, sandy soils. It is very tolerant of wind exposure, due to its thick, resilient leaves, but is frost-sensitive, though not usually fatally so. If the tree planter is prepared to suffer pain in the name of successful establishment, trees planted in gaps in gorse clumps will be naturally protected from browsing by deer and livestock, though not from rabbits. The trees will also have a readily available source of nitrogen, as gorse is a nitrogen-fixing species. The succession from heath to gorse, and then to trees such as birch and rowan and beyond, is a natural one across the whole of Britain.

Stratified seed that was collected in August and September will germinate freely if sown outside in the spring, or in pots in a cold frame. Side-shoots taken in midsummer can also be used for propagation, by inserting them in compost in a cold frame, and keeping them moist.

Gorse used to be planted as hedges and windbreaks for livestock as it is thick enough to be impenetrable to cattle, but is still semi-permeable to the wind. It is also very good cover for birds as the thorns protect linnets, whinchats and the now rare Dartford warbler.

The bushes used to be planted near dwellings for hanging washing on. Gorse was also used extensively as fuel, either as faggots, particularly for bakers' ovens in England, or made into charcoal. The flowers provide a welcome early pasture for bees and the crushed stems were fed to horses. This supposedly caused them to grow the long whiskers that are so noticeable on heavy, working breeds.

In medicinal terms, gorse was commonly used to control heartburn as it contains the same *isoliquiritigenen* as is found in liquorice. The dose would have had to be carefully controlled, however, as gorse contains the same poisons as laburnum. A decoction of the flowers was used to cure jaundice and gall-stones. The almond and honey scent, reminiscent of coconut, is still used today in men's toiletries.

The saying 'When gorse is out of bloom, kissing's out of season', or versions of it, are found all over the British Isles, including Scotland.

Guelder Rose

This shrub has many different names, including Water-elder, Love-rose, and Pincushion Tree but there seems to be little or no folklore attached to it, despite the fact that it is probably native to much of Britain.

The guelder rose (*Viburnum opulus*) is part of the *Caprifoliaceae* family, which contains the honeysuckles, elders, and the wayfaring tree. The name is actually taken from the sterile form, also known as the snowberry, which was introduced to Britain from Guelderland in the Netherlands about 400 years ago.

It is naturally widespread in Britain, growing on wet ground, especially on woodland edges. It is a common part of the flora of oak woodland, and on boggy ground grows alongside alder buckthorn, sallow, birch, and alder. It is generally a lowland shrub but can sometimes be found on the fringes of upland forests in N.W Scotland.

A large, spreading shrub, up to 4m in height, the guelder rose has surprisingly few branches. Its drooping, bright red berries are often retained long after the elder-like leaves (which turn a loganberry red in autumn) have been shed. The fertile forms have a ring of large, white, sterile but insect-attracting flowers, together with smaller, white, fertile ones. The cultivated snow-berry tree has lost the fertile ones and retains the others in tight clusters, which then form white berries, hence the name. the leaves, berries and bark of both trees are poisonous, although guelder rose berries can be rendered safe by cooking. This is said not to be worth trying, as they do not taste good.

Guelder rose rarely lives to an extended age when grown in gardens but in the wild specimens with stem girths of more than half a metre have been observed.

Guelder rose should be planted on wet sites, preferably on the periphery of woodlands and forests. It is especially useful for sites where oak is one of the major component species, and in conjunction with those species already mentioned as being its natural neighbours. Seed should be collected in September and October, and planted in the spring in pots in a cold frame or glasshouse. Vegetative propagation by layering is also successful, and is essential for the sterile forms.

There are few modern uses for guelder rose because of its poisonous nature, although a tincture made from its bark is a remedy for menstrual and post-partum cramps. In prehistoric times it was used for arrows, one of which was discovered in an Aberdeenshire peat bog in the 19th C.

The guelder rose is the national symbol of the Ukraine and figures extensively in its creation mythology. There its berries symbolise blood and undying traces of family roots. In Scotland there seems to be no associated lore.

Gorse and Guelder Rose: Rob Pile
BSc (Hons), DipLA, CMLI, Tech.Arbor.A
Forestry Contracts Manager, Nicholson's Nurseries,
Bicester, Oxford.

Other bushes: Martin Howard

CHERRY
Prunus avium and P. padus / Fhioghag

The two cherries native to Scotland are the gean, also known as the mazzard, or simply the wild cherry (*Prunus avium*), and the bird cherry, or wild black cherry (*Prunus padus*). The botanical names don't help us to remember them, as they seem to apply to the wrong ones! In fact they are both favourites with birds, which eat them greedily and help to disperse the stones. Gean is one of the ancestors of our garden and orchard cherries. The Gaelic name *Fhioghag* is not very illuminating, as it refers to a fig.

Where it grows

The natural range of wild cherry includes the whole of Europe as far north as Scandinavia, and extends into western Asia and North Africa. It occurs throughout Scotland but is less common in the north, and grows best on rich, freely drained, lowland soils.

Bird cherry has a similar but more upland distribution and is found right up to northern Scandinavia. In Britain, unlike gean which is frequent in southern beechwoods, bird cherry is common only in northern England and Scotland and is rare in the south.

Gean can hardly be described as common in Scotland, but forms a minor part of mixed broadleaved woods, along with oak and ash on the better soils. Its distribution is not as natural as that of bird cherry, as there has been much planting of gean over the centuries for amenity and for timber. I suspect bird cherry has largely been left to its own devices. Since birds drop cherry stones almost at random, gean especially can spring up in unexpected places as a single tree. However, gean suckers strongly, much as aspen does, and, in the right conditions, will establish a small clone or group of small trees around it. It also coppices, although this has not been an important management technique for gean.

In woodland conditions bird cherry can be locally abundant in upland wet-flushed areas, often in association with alder, but it is also common on roadsides and alongside burns in the glens.

What to look for

In good woodland conditions gean can be a tall tree, up to 30m in height, but in Scotland it is usually less, depending on soil conditions and degree of exposure. Young trees have regular branching in whorls with a single main stem, making it a popular tree with foresters, as it also responds to pruning and thinning.

However, gean was not planted extensively until the 1950s and it rarely dominates a woodland canopy. Neither is it common in hedgerows, despite its ability to coppice and sucker. It really is a tree that does best in mixed woods and is not suitable for pure planted blocks, partly because of its susceptibility to cherry canker and honey fungus. There are a number of other diseases in cherry, and leaf scorch has been a concern in England. Fortunately, however, cherry is almost immune to damage from grey squirrels.

Gean bark is purplish-brown, initially smooth with a shine, but becoming ridged and furrowed with age, whilst still retaining lenticels in characteristic horizontal stripes. Bird cherry bark is blackish and finely grained. Both cherries can exude quantities of clear resinous gum to protect wounds on the stem. Gean leaves are long and oval, with long crimson stalks and toothed edges, ending in points. Pale green at first, appearing just after the white blossom, they darken to mid-green but in autumn provide many colours from yellow though to deep red.

Bird cherry leaves remain a paler green and are more finely toothed, while the buds are oval and pointed but more slender than gean. The white flowers hanging in clusters on long spikes can be even more spectacular than gean, although less widely recognised. Bird cherry fruits are blacker than gean's dark-red cherries and are known in parts of Scotland as 'hags', giving the shrub the name 'hag cherry'. Bird cherry rarely grows much larger than a multi-stemmed bush of up to 15m.

Where to plant

Gean likes deep, moist, freely draining loams and is frost hardy. It does not do very well, though it may survive, in exposed situations or in poor, peaty, acid soils. However, there are often niches in many upland planting sites which would take a small group of gean, especially where its attractive blossom will one day be appreciated. It could be used much more extensively in mixed plantings with oak and ash to help restock lowland woods where wych elm has been eliminated by disease.

Bird cherry will tolerate poorer, wetter soils and greater exposure but again is more likely to do well on locally better soils in more sheltered sites such as burn-sides. Planting should be limited to small groups or individuals in fairly open areas.

Cultivation

Cherries produce viable seed at an early age and at intervals of three to five years. Gean and bird cherry seeds are ready for collecting from July to September after the fruits turn red and black respectively. Try to collect from genuinely native trees rather than those which have obviously been planted, as 20 or 30 years ago much stock was imported from Continental Europe.

The seeds can either be sown immediately or the following spring, after treatment. After collection, the stones should be separated from the pulp and stratified in a compost of moist, sieved peat and sand or soil. They germinate best if given a two-week warm period, followed by an 18-week cold period. Seedlings should reach 10–15cm at the end of the first year and may be lined out after one or two years.

Cherry usually takes well after transplanting and puts on rapid growth (well above average for broadleaves), provided weeds are controlled in the first two years. Although cherries will respond to tree shelters, height growth can be very good without them. Shelters or spiral guards may be necessary to protect them from deer or rabbit damage, however.

Uses

The timber of gean is particularly hard and fine, with a light brown heartwood and paler sapwood. It is in demand for furniture, turnery, and musical instruments. Highland-grown gean can have a green stain, seen as degrading its quality in the trade, but which can add interest in individual, locally made furniture. Timber strength is comparable with that of oak, but cherry is less likely to split.

If the trees have been pruned early in their life, knots are reduced and timber becomes more valuable for furniture. Bird cherry has a similar but paler wood. It rarely reaches timber size, though it could be used in turnery and crafts. The young stems are tough and have been used in the past for barrel bands or cooperage rings.

The attractive spring flowers, the crop of cherries – for birds and, in good fruiting years, for people – make this an appealing tree. Excellent liqueurs can be made from both types of cherry, as well as jam or jelly. These *Fhioghag*, with the valuable timber, make the two native cherries very much worth growing more widely in Scotland.

Lore

The bird cherry is said not to have a folklore of its own. Over most of the seasons it is unobtrusive, and yet is very noticeable twice in the year: once when it produces its showy spikes of white flowers in May, and again when it is covered with the silky webs of the bird cherry ermine moth in late June.

Like several other attractive trees in the Highlands, gean has a superstition preventing its being cut and it is a herald of fate, good or bad, when one comes across it. However, I suspect that the folk in the east, where it is more common, would have taken full advantage of its fine timber.

Peter Quelch

was Scottish Native Woodland Advisor for the Forestry Commission and, more recently, Bio-diversity Advisor. He spends his retirement milling timber and contributing to woodland projects in Argyll.

Sources

Prior, S.N., *The silviculture and yield of wild cherry*. Forestry Commission Bulletin 75, 1988.

Gordon, A.G. and Rowe, D.C.F., *Seed manual for ornamental trees and shrubs*. Forestry Commission Bulletin 59, 1982.

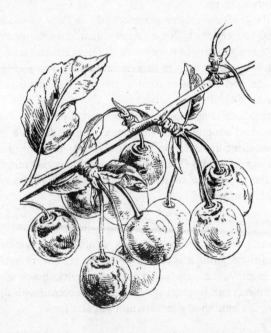

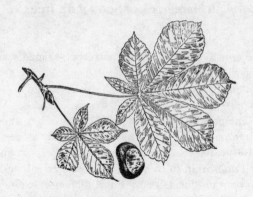

CHESTNUT
Castanea sativa and Aesculus hippocastanum

There are two species of trees known as chestnut commonly found in Scotland, which, although not native, have a broad, if scattered, distribution. These are the sweet chestnut (*Castanea sativa*) and the horse chestnut (*Aesculus hippocastanum*). They are completely unrelated.

Where it grows

The natural distribution of sweet, or Spanish, chestnut is limited to Mediterranean countries, including Spain, Morocco, Italy, Greece, Turkey and France. The Romans introduced it to Britain two thousand years ago, as the nuts were a staple food for their legionaries. The British climate, however, was not quite conducive to good chestnut harvests. Although the tree can ripen fertile seeds in the south of England, where it reproduces naturally, from the Midlands north it tends to be seen only as an ornamental specimen tree, artificially sown and planted. For all that, it will grow well even in the far north-east of Scotland. There is a very old specimen, planted in 1550, still growing near Strathpeffer, east Ross.

Horse chestnut is a common parkland and garden tree. It is only found naturally in Albania and Greece, but was introduced here in 1616. The name is said to derive from the practice of feeding the nuts to ailing horses, as they contain a substance known as aesculin, which relieves muscular strains and bruises.

It could equally come from the horseshoe-shaped scars left on the twigs when leaves are shed.

What to look for

A very fine parkland tree, the sweet chestnut has smooth, grey bark on young trees, which fissures vertically as they mature. After 100 years the fissures and ridges become more pronounced and begin to twist spirally. The tree is long-lived and can grow up to 35m tall and 3m in diameter. It also coppices well and, as a forest tree, the species has most value when managed in this way. In summer the large, long oval leaves are very distinctive, and in winter the tree can be recognised by its stout twigs, which are angular and marked by ridges. The nuts are produced in October in spiny husks, each consisting of four bracts that enclose up to three brown nuts. In Scotland these are only occasionally plump and worth eating, and even then, they will be smaller than those found in the south.

The horse chestnut is grown solely for ornament and is a fine parkland or avenue tree. The bark is greyish brown and as it ages it breaks up into rough squares. The trunks of old trees often become ribbed or fluted and appear pinkish-brown. It can achieve similar dimensions to the sweet chestnut but its structure is markedly less strong, and older trees can shed heavy branches. Its leaves are a distinctive palmate shape, with between three and seven, but usually five, leaflets. In winter its stout twigs set heavy ovate buds covered in resin ('sticky buds') to protect against insect attack.

The white flower spikes (pink in some cultivars) are a magnificent sight when they open in May. These are followed by the spiky green husks of the fruits, which are more fleshy than those of the sweet chestnut, within which develop the familiar horse chestnuts, or conkers. The leaves turn a spectacular range of yellows and reds at the start of autumn.

Where to plant

Neither tree is appropriate for native woodland planting schemes, but they have a place in parks, gardens and general woodland. Sweet chestnut needs a moderately fertile soil and does best in a mild climate. Although it can cope with a low pH, it is unsuitable for frosty or exposed sites on poorly drained ground and, in Scotland, should only be planted on the best sites. On light soils it is liable to dry out. Shakes tend to develop and to become a problem in older trees.

Horse chestnut requires a similarly fertile soil, but it is more tolerant of heavy ground conditions and frost. Again, if the species is to be planted as a small part of a scheme, care must be taken with site selection. In recent years horse chestnuts have fallen prey to two ailments: the leaf miner, *Cameraria ohridella*, and a fungal (or possibly a bacterial) pathogen causing stem bleeding, commonly known as bleeding canker.

Cultivation

Sweet chestnut is easily raised from seed, provided the nuts are carefully stored away from rodents, and not allowed to dry out or become mouldy. Moist sand is a good storage medium. The tree will produce a good seed crop after 30 to 40 years, and this is best collected in October. A warm, late summer is required to ripen the nuts, and only the biggest ones are worth collecting.

Horse chestnut is also easy to propagate, provided that the seeds are stored in moist conditions all winter through. The whole nut remains below ground and sends up a stout shoot that bears compound leaves right from the outset. Good seed crops occur after only 20 years, and these should also be collected in October.

Uses

Sweet chestnut timber is very strong and its heartwood naturally durable. Along with oak, it is the only widely grown hardwood that is suitable to use untreated for outside work such as fencing and building. Its value as timber, however, is severely reduced by its tendency to shake or crack, particularly in older trees where both ring and star shakes occur, making it difficult to produce large planks. Uses of sawn timber include furniture and coffin boards. Its greatest value is grown as coppice, as it is in the south of England. Grown on a rotation of 12 to 15 years, it can produce poles with a high proportion of heartwood, which are cleft by hand to make pales. These are bound together with wire to use as fencing, or used individually as stakes. The fruits are also valuable, roasted chestnuts being traditional English fare. The skins should be split and the nuts put in the ash of a hot fire, leaving one uncut. When it explodes, the others are ready! The nuts can be cooked in a variety of ways, both in sweet and savoury dishes. Care should be taken when trying to store chestnuts, as they dry out easily.

Horse chestnut timber is completely different, being white and pulpy and not strong. It has no real commercial value, although it has occasionally been used as shelving for apples and pears and for making toys. The nuts are also useful for little but schoolchildren's duels, but work has been carried out on the medicinal properties of their aesculin component.

Martin Howard

CRAB APPLE
Malus sylvestris

The name 'crab' derives from the Norse *skrab*, meaning 'small and rough' (tree), closely akin to the Scots 'scribe' and 'scrub' as in 'willow-scrub'. In the Borders crab apples are still referred to as 'scrogs', another descendant of the Norse word. The word 'apple' is similar in all the Celtic, Germanic and Scandinavian languages.

What to look for

The crab apple is a shrub or small tree up to 10m high with thorny branches, faintly pink flowers and almost-round fruit, which are about 2.5cm in diameter, glossy pale green (but flushed red when mature) and dimpled at both ends. Leaves are alternate, ovate to broadly elliptical, short-pointed and serrated. Crab apple comes into leaf in late April, flowers in May, and the fruit ripens in October.

Crab apple or cultivated apple?

It can be difficult to distinguish a crab apple from the 'wilding' or seedling 'escape' of the cultivated apple, *Malus domestica*, due to the great variability of cultivated apples. The only definitive way to identify a crab apple is in the glabrous (smooth) nature of the upper surface of the mature leaf, the pedicels and the outside of the calyx of the crab when compared with the domestic apple.

Until recently, it was commonly supposed that the crab apple was an important ancestor of the domestic apple, but the most recent work has shown this to be incorrect. Using DNA testing, Barry Juniper of the University of Oxford has shown that the edible domestic apple is a descendent of *Malus sieversii*, a native of Tien Shan, on the border between China and Kazakhstan. However, according to Joan Morgan, the crab apple is probably an ancestor of certain cider apples. The flowering crab apples, which are grown mainly for ornamental purposes, are derived from a variety of sources including the wild crab apple.

There are 93 insect species known to be associated with the crab apple.

Where it grows

Crab apple is native throughout Europe, and related species are found throughout the temperate zone of the northern hemisphere. Although there are isolated examples of crab apples in the north of Scotland, it is only considered to be a native species in southern Scotland. Nowhere is it common, and it can occur singly or scattered throughout almost all types of woodland. It prefers neutral or slightly alkaline soil and will only tolerate slight shade.

Cultivation

The fruits should be picked as soon as they are ripe, in October or November, before they are all eaten by birds. Cut the apples up immediately and extract the pips by hand, or float them off the pulp in water. The seed must then be sown or stratified (mixed with soil or sand and kept moist over the winter) immediately and should be protected from mice and squirrels. Stratified seed should be sown in trays or seedbeds, and lightly covered with sand. Depending on density, the seeds can be lined out in the first summer, or after one growing season. Crab apples can also be propagated from stools, roots, or suckers by layering.

Uses

The fruit makes one of the best jellies of all wild fruits, either alone or mixed with rowanberries. It can also make a good cider. 'Verjuice' is fermented, concentrated juice, which medieval cooks used much as we use lemon juice today. The fruit can also be roasted and served with meat, or added to winter punches and warmed ale. With the addition of spices, the latter, known as 'lamb's wool', was mentioned by Shakespeare.

Timber quality is excellent, being hard and close-grained, and if dried very slowly is suitable for fine carving and engraving. It is, however, difficult to work, but is easily stained and polished. It also makes good firewood with a pleasant aroma, and is particularly good for smoking fish or meat. In the past it was used to make wooden screws, cam wheels, mallets, and other items requiring hardness and strength.

Crab apple is one of the Bach flower remedies, being known as the 'cleansing remedy'. Its main use is to assist those who feel they have something 'unclean' or 'poisonous' about them.

Lore

Did Eve really bite into an apple that she had plucked off the forbidden tree of knowledge of good and evil in the garden of Eden? No specific name is given to the fruit she tasted from that tree, though apples are mentioned later in the Bible. Some historians believe that Eve's fruit may have been a pomegranate, or even a quince.

There is a variety of folklore associated with apples, mostly to do with true love, and determining the suitability of marriage partners. A typical example is the throwing of apple pips into the fire while saying the name of your lover. If the pip explodes, then love is true; if not, the pip will burn quietly away.

John Butterworth
ran an organic fruit nursery near Cumnock for many years. He is still a leading authority on Scottish fruit trees.

Sources
Lang, D.C., *The Complete Book of British Berries*. Threshold Books, 1967.
Price, E., *East of Eden in The Garden*. The Royal Horticultural Society, 2001.
Morgan, J., *The Book of Apples*. Ebury Press, 1993.

DOG ROSE
Rosa canina

Many people think of roses as large, many-petalled flowers or bushes with growth forms artificially adapted to various situations in the garden. Unless they are lovers of the countryside, they probably dismiss the native wild roses as prickly plants that make a short show of flowers in early summer. If they name them at all, they are apt to lump them all together as 'dog roses'. There are, in fact, twelve native species of *Rosa*. Until recently, amateur botanists, and even many of the professionals, neglected the study of wild roses, finding a bewildering array of varieties and forms, which discouraged attempts at identification. There are two main reasons for this. First, roses hybridise freely; almost any species can pollinate any other and produce hybrids of varying degrees of fertility. Secondly, roses of the section *Caninae* have a peculiar and almost unique method of reproduction, which complicates the issue even more. However, recent research has clarified the taxonomic difficulties, making it easier to distinguish the species, so that more people are taking an interest in the wild roses.

British wild roses

The British rose occurs in two main forms: upright bushes with more or less straight stems, which are strong enough to stand erect, even without support, or climbing roses with weak, arching *stems* which require support from other plants, such as hedgerow bushes. All are deciduous, with pinnate leaves having five to eleven leaflets. The flowers, with five petals, range from pure white through pink to deep red. After flowering, the receptacle, or end of the flower stalk, becomes deeply concave, forming a fleshy structure, the rose hip, which is a false fruit, totally enclosing the hard, true fruits.

Where they grow and what to look for

Six of the native British species have a southern distribution and do not occur in Scotland, except possibly as occasional introductions. These are *Rosa arvensis, R. stylosa, R. obtusifolia, R. tomentosa, R. micrantha,* and *R. agrestis.*

The burnet rose (*R. pimpernellifolia*) is an erect shrub, rarely more than a metre high, with usually 11 small leaflets to each leaf, purplish-black hips and masses of nearly straight, sharp prickles. It spreads freely by suckers and forms dense, impenetrable masses over large areas. Its main habitat throughout the country is coastal sand dunes, but it also occurs inland on calcareous soils.

The true dog rose, *R. canina,* is very common throughout the British Isles but is more frequent in the south. In Scotland the northern dog roses, *R. caesia* subspecies *caesia* and *vosagiaca,* are more frequent than *R. canina,* especially on higher ground.

The downy roses have very hairy leaves and glands on the leaves and elsewhere, which give a resinous odour when crushed. The two species native in Scotland are both erect, self-supporting shrubs. Sherard's downy rose (*R. sheradii*) has flexuous, slightly zigzag stems. The soft downy rose (*R. mollis*) has straight stems and perfectly straight prickles. It suckers freely and so can form dense thickets. *Rosa rubiginosa,* sweet briar or eglantine, is one of the three British species that have a fruity odour resembling apples. It is an erect, straight-stemmed plant. On a warm, still day its fruity smell can be detected several metres away.

There are also numerous hybrids involving these native species in varying degrees of complexity, so that some guidance is needed before one can become familiar with one's local rose species. In addition, there are a few alien species, which sometimes appear in the wild as escapes from cultivation. The commonest of these is the Japanese rose (*R. rugosa*) which is frequently planted in landscaping schemes and may appear spontaneously elsewhere, especially on coastal sand dunes. It spreads by suckering and has large, strongly scented flowers and very large hips.

Cultivation

If one wants to grow a particular species of wild rose, one cannot rely on growing it from seed. *Rosa* species hybridise so readily that there is no knowing what will appear when the seeds germinate.

With two native species, both of which occur in Scotland, there is an easy way of obtaining young plants. The Burnet rose (*R. pimpernellifolia*) and the soft downy rose (*R. mollis*) both produce suckers, complete with their own roots, and these can easily be detached from their parents. Most other species produce fresh shoots from the base, which can be rooted, but which are not easily detached without damaging the main bush.

Cuttings can be taken from the first or second year's wood. In my experience, this has been a chancy business. Sometimes nearly all my cuttings have struck and on other occasions I have not succeeded in raising a single one. However, I am an irregular and inexperienced gardener and no doubt people more expert than I would be more successful.

For anyone wishing to introduce native rose species into natural habitats, two warnings may be appropriate. First of all, make sure that the species you intend to introduce are suitable for the local climate and soil. The descriptions of the species above will show which naturally occur in Scotland, and hence which ones are likely to succeed here. Roses do not tolerate very wet soil and, except for possibly *R. sheradii* and *R. mollis*, do not thrive in acid soil. Some species, notably *R rubiginosa*, need a calcareous soil.

The second warning is that as a general rule it is unwise to try to obtain 'wild' roses from nurseries. These establishments provide an excellent service for garden roses, but very few nursery people have an intimate knowledge of British wild roses. Thus, for example, specimens of *R. pimpernellifolia* or *R. rubignosa*, which are usually obtainable from nurseries, will almost certainly be garden cultivars with many differences from the true wild plants. The 'wild roses' obtained from nurseries for landscaping schemes are often incongruous mixtures of dubious cultivars quite unsuited to the region or soil in which they are planted. Obtain your roses from the wild, but remember the law, which lays down that wild plants of any sort may not be uprooted without the consent of the owner of the land.

Uses

Roses are mainly valued for the beauty of their flowers, their scent, and the contribution they make to the adornment of gardens and public places. The burnet rose, with its suckering habit, is of value in stabilising coastal sand dunes with its dense colonies. The hips of wild roses are an important source of food for birds. They are also very rich in Vitamin C, and were collected during the Second World War and made into rose-hip syrup. Dried rose hips can be made into tea by infusing them with boiling water in a thermos flask. They must be left for three or four hours in the flask, and the resulting tea is delicious. Rose petals are also a constituent of pot pourri.

Lore

Roses appear in literature more frequently than virtually any other plants, especially in poetry. The description of a red rose in Pliny's *Natural History* (AD 79) is sufficiently detailed to identify it as the present day species *R. gallica*. The emblems of the contending factions in the Wars of the Roses were not native British species, but two garden plants. The white rose of York is *Rosa alba,* and the red rose of Lancaster is *Rosa gallica*. One of the legends concerning roses is that of St Elizabeth of Hungary. She was carrying an apron full of bread to feed the poor when her husband, who disapproved of her charitable activities, demanded to know what she was holding. She unfolded her apron and it was full of roses.

Dr A. L. Primavesi (D. Sc.)

(d. 2011) was a Botanical Society referee for British roses and co-author of the Society's guide to native roses.

Sources

Graham, G.G. and Primavesi A.L., *Roses of Great Britain and Ireland*. BSBI Handbook No 7, Botanical Society of the British Isles, 1991.
Stace, C.A., *New Flora of the British Isles*. Cambridge, 1991.

DOUGLAS FIR
Pseudotsuga menziesii (Mirbel) Franco

Douglas fir was originally known as Oregon pine, a name still used by many. Both the current names, common and scientific, refer to Scottish plant hunters. David Douglas was born at Scone in 1799, the son of a stonemason. He worked as a gardener at Scone and later at the Glasgow Botanic Gardens. On behalf of the London Horticultural Society he explored the north-west American coast from 1823–32, bringing back more than 200 species of plants, making him the greatest of all botanical explorers. He brought Douglas fir seed to Scotland in around 1826. However, the species had actually been 'discovered' (of course it was already known to the indigenous population) in around 1791 by another Scot, Dr Archibald Menzies, surgeon and botanist on Captain Vancouver's expedition in the area. Douglas fir's scientific name, *Pseudotsuga menziesii*, acknowledges Menzies' role. The American practice of hyphenating the name as Douglas-fir is commendable as it emphasises that it is not one of the fifty or so species of true fir.

What to look for

Douglas fir is one of the easiest conifers to identify. Before we became interested in trees, any of us would doubtless have been able to recognise from our younger days say, oak, holly, horse chestnut and monkey puzzle. All other trees, if we noticed them at all, were a bit of a mystery, appearing to us just as different shades of green. Then we found that the crushed foliage of a particular evergreen gives off the aroma of oranges, and at the same time there are vertical, orange striations in its bark. The ground around it is littered with cones, each with small, three-cornered bracts protruding from under the scales. This turned out to be the Douglas fir. True, the crushed foliage of the unrelated Grand fir (*Abies grandis*) has a somewhat similar kind of aroma – but that is more like tangerines. Also, a further species has orange fissures in its bark, the much rarer Low's white fir (*Abies concolor* var. *lowiana*), but Low's white foliage is usually high, with longer needles, and cones on the ground are very rare. The abundance of cones on the ground tells us that our tree is not in the silver fir (*Abies*) group; the extruding bracts tell us that it is not a spruce either; and the flat, soft foliage shows us we do not have a pine.

The buds, unlike those of any other conifer, are like beech buds, sharply pointed and shiny brown. When young, Douglas fir is of conical form, only taking its narrower form after a few decades. Both sexes of cone are on the same tree, maturing over one season, and usually becoming ripe by early August. Leaves are 15–35mm long, either blunt or acute tipped, dark-green or bluish-green above and a lighter green underneath, with two whitish stomata lines. The smooth, dark bark of young trees resembles that of various other conifers, with the usual resin blisters; it is only after a few decades that the distinctive orange cracks appear.

Where it grows

In various forms, the Douglas fir ranges from Mexico to British Columbia, from the coast to about 3000m above sea level, taking in a wide variety of conditions. It thrives on moist, well-drained soils; on chalky soils, foliage is yellow and sickly. It is the USA's number one tree for lumber and timber volume and is one of the world's foremost timber species. Along with other conifers, like Sitka spruce (*Picea sitchensis*), coast redwood (*Sequoia sempervirens*), and giant redwood (*Sequoiadendron giganteum*), it is one of the giants of the west coast of America. At one time, Douglas fir was the world's tallest conifer at over 120m (topping the current record coast redwoods at 112m) but those particular trees were felled. Ages of over 1400 years have been achieved, with a girth of almost 14m in Washington State, where the author has also seen fossilised *Pseudotsuga*. The best specimens are those nearest the coast, where there is a high humidity.

Douglas fir can form pure stands but is more usually found growing with other conifers. It can have a flattened top if it has grown faster than its ability to raise water by capillary action. The thick, resinous bark, which can be up to 60cm thick, is for fire protection, but in its native area, natural stands of Douglas fir need fire, or other interventions such as blow-down, to prevent western hemlock (*Tsuga heterophyllia*) from taking over. Preferred annual precipitation ranges from about 40cm inland and upland, to about 250cm at the coast, and temperatures as low as -40°C can be tolerated.

When brought into Europe, Douglas fir soon became the tallest tree, surpassing the silver fir. Here in the British Isles, Douglas fir is usually neck and neck with Sitka spruce and grand fir, one of the current tallest standing at around 64m in Reelig Glen, Moniack, near Inverness. Elsewhere in Scotland we have some equally awesome specimens, whether out in the open and thus multi-branched, or at river level in a glen, thus reaching up for light. One of the trees from the original import is at Drumlanrig, near Thornhill, Dumfries and Galloway, from seed gifted when Douglas' brother was employed there.

Forms and related species

There are some twenty recognised different kinds of *Pseudotsuga* (including four species, three varieties, and a number of cultivars). The genus is found in both eastern Asia (Japan, China and Taiwan) and as well as north-western America. As with certain other genera, this Asia/America axis is possibly the result of continental drift.

There is a variety, blue Douglas fir (*P.m. var glauca*), on the eastern Rockies, that differs in several ways. The tree is notably smaller and the foliage shorter, thicker and bluer. Introduced about 1884, it is an uncommon tree in Britain. The other American species with a more restricted distribution is bigcone spruce (*P. macrocarpa*), from the mountains of California. It reaches about 1m in girth and 25m in height and is mainly used for fuel. The comparatively large cone can be almost 20cm long.

Diseases

Severe dieback comes from *Phomopsis pseudotsugae* and foliage discoloration is the result of *Rhabdoclyne pseudotsugae*. Extreme dampness or crowding can lead to grey mould (*Botritis cinerea*), while the principal insect pest is *Adelges cooleyi*.

Uses

The timber can be variable in colour, yellowish and/or reddish-brown even in the same tree. It is moderately durable and fairly hard. Wide, unknotted boards are a feature, making it increasingly sought-after in the building trade. In the past it has been used for pit-props, bridges, boats, masts, flagpoles, rolling stock, posts and general heavy-duty applications.

John Miller

is a life member of the International Dendrology Society. He is Curator Of Trees at several Highland estates; also author of *Trees of the Northern Highlands* and of *Trees Of Glasgow*.

ELDER
Sambucus

The name 'elder' comes from the Anglo-Saxon *ellaern* and is probably related to the word 'hollow', from the character of the trees' smaller stems. The Scots name, *bourtree* (bore-tree) conveys the same idea. This feature made the elder a useful tree for the construction of bellows and musical instruments. The generic name *Sambucus* originates from the Greek *sambuke*, meaning 'flute'. In England elder was often planted outside homes to keep malignant spirits away, much as rowan is in Scotland. Gifts of milk and cakes were sometimes offered to secure this protection. This probably connects with the northern European belief that elder was the home of an old woman, Dame Ellhorn. In Lincolnshire there are still those who will not cut down an elder without 'asking the old lady's leave'.

Where it grows

Common elder (*Sambucus nigra*) belongs to the honeysuckle family (*Caprifoliaceae*), which includes three other British natives: Guelder rose, Wayfaring Tree, and Honeysuckle itself. It is the only small *Sambucus* genus native to Britain, although its cousin, red-berried elder, *Sambucus racemosa*, is locally common in south-east Scotland and the north of England. The natural distribution of the native elder extends across the whole country except for the most north-westerly islands. Its natural range is thought to cover most of Europe, the Caucasus, Asia Minor, and western Siberia.

Palaeological studies suggest that elder was a relative latecomer to these islands, reaching the north of Scotland as recently as 2000 years ago.

What to look for

Rarely exceeding 6m in height, elder is more frequently thought of as a shrub than a tree. Its general form – leaning and twisting trunk, fissured bark, spreading crown, pale grey and orange shoots and suckers – and its compact size give it a value as an ornamental shrub and explain its frequent occurrence in parks and gardens. It is also a rapid colonist of disturbed places, such as railway verges and demolition sites.

It is probably for its clusters of tiny, sweet-scented cream flowers that elder is most commonly valued. The bisexual flowers of May and June turn by September into berries, well known for their deep, rich purple colour. Elder is often one of the earliest native shrubs to come into leaf, its fresh green shoots being a welcome sight in January or February when nothing else is flushing. A severe late frost may damage the young shoots, but this seems to have no effect on flowering and fruiting. In traditional country lore, the opening of the flowers marks the season for seed sowing.

Annual shoots are green with many prominent grey lenticels and have an almost herbaceous appearance. They may occasionally be killed by frost in winter but generally survive to become permanent stems. Branches have a soft, pithy centre, while the main stems are composed of a heavy, hard and very strong wood, which is yellowish-white in colour, with no distinct heartwood.

Where to plant

Although it is a fairly adaptable species, elder prefers a deep, moist but well-drained, nitrogenous soil. It is known to be tolerant of both air and soil pollution, and is often found growing near refuse and rotting organic waste. This latter observation led the Saxons to avoid it, as they believed it could only grow where human blood had been spilt! It dislikes both excessive light and deep shade and therefore is found most commonly as a shrub-layer in light forest stands.

Cultivation

Elder is a prolific seed producer and is spread naturally by birds and badgers. It also has the ability to spread by root suckers. Sowing seed is possible, but the fleshy fruit can be difficult to handle and bird predation is a common problem.

Vegetative propagation is therefore the preferred method. This can be carried out by inserting half-ripened shoots in a frame in late summer. These should be removed from the shrub with a short 'heel' of older wood attached. Alternatively, in the back end, 15cm cuttings of the previous year's growth can be planted to a depth of about 7–8cm in the open ground.

Uses

Although rarely used today, the hardwood was once valued for a variety of household artefacts such as bowls and forks. It is still said to be the best material for making wooden spoons.

The leaves, berries and bark have been used in Scotland for making dye, and still are by a few individuals. Medicinal uses include elderflower tea, which has a sudorific (sweat-inducing) effect and is considered to be an effective remedy for the common cold. The berries are high in Vitamin C and are also said to have an anti-viral effect, making elderberry tea a useful 'flu remedy. Made into a syrup, they can be used to ease sore throats, or they can be made into jams and jellies, particularly in combination with apples or crab apples.

Elderflowers are used commercially to make a refreshing summer drink, while wine is made, from both the flowers and the fruit, commercially and at home. The strong-smelling and rather rank foliage was formerly used for repelling insects and their associated germs. Even today, some country people in England still retain the custom of wearing elder leaves in their hair or clothing when out walking or working. In Scotland, the associations seem to have been different:

> *Bourtree, bourtree, crooked rung,*
> *Never straight and never strong*
> *Ever bush and never tree*
> *Since our Lord was nailed to ye.*

Tess Darwin, however, suggests that this was a transference to Christian mythology of an older pagan association with death.

Consider planting elder to provide shelter and food for birds and animals as well as crops for human harvest.

Eamonn Wall and Alastair Seaman

are both woodland design consultants with Eamonn Wall & Co. in Dollar.

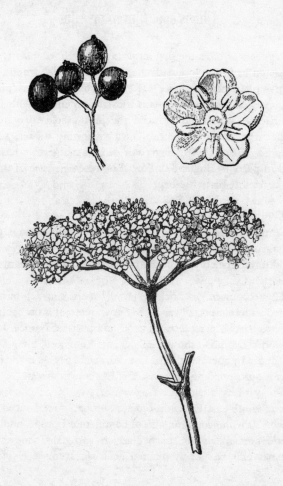

ELM
Ulmus spp. / Leven or Ailm

Elm appears as *ailm*, the first letter in the Gaelic alphabet, and is associated in Celtic lore with the dead and burial grounds. The Scottish place-name *leamhain* (Leven) probably means 'place of the elms'. The future of elms is inextricably linked with Dutch elm disease, which has reduced the proud field-edge trees of southern Britain to no more than low-growing suckers since it appeared in the 1960s. Regrowth of elm hedgerows has been rapid in parts of England, followed by re-emergence of the disease and subsequent die-back.

Distribution

It seems likely that the only representative of the genus *Ulmus* that is truly native to Scotland is the Wych elm (*Ulmus glabra*). It would have formed part of the climax woodland in many areas of Scotland.

The common, or English, elm (*Ulmus procera*) has been planted widely, especially as a hedgerow tree, but is probably only native to parts of southern England and parts of France. It does not readily hybridise and is rarely grown from seed, but generally reproduces by suckering. This last characteristic has made it particularly susceptible to the ravages of Dutch elm disease.

Smooth-leaved elm (*U. carpinifolia*) was once common in parts of south-east England, but was probably introduced there early on. It is the common elm of continental Europe, and many varieties are familiar here, particularly the fastigiate (cone-shaped) Wheatley elm, frequently planted in urban avenues. Hybrids of the smooth-leaved elm and the Wych elm give rise to the Dutch elm (*U.x hollandicia, var. hollandicia*) and the noble Huntingdon elm (*U. x hollandicia var. vegeta*). These are believed to be naturally occurring hybrids, the Huntingdon being discovered near the Cambridgeshire town in 1750. It is one of the finest elms and was commonly planted in Scottish parks and gardens.

Scotland's unique elm is the Camperdown elm (*U. glabra Camperdownii*). In summer its compact, umbrella-shaped crown supports rivulets of pendulous foliage which mask tortuously convoluted branches. These are only visible from under the canopy. The tree is commonly grafted on to straight Wych elm stock, all originals having arisen from one original and still-surviving parent in Camperdown Park, Dundee.

The mature wych elm can be a magnificently tall and colossally broad-domed tree, which may reach 40m tall and 7m in girth. The Latin *glabra* refers to the appearance of the bark in the young tree: smooth and grey. The adult has dark brown or grey bark that is vertically fissured. Major branches may be present low down on the stem, giving rise to the broad crown.

The trunk and branches are often burred. The shoots are stout, with dull, red-brown buds. In early spring, small purplish-red flowers emerge, followed by the large, pale-green seed that browns and is cast to the wind in early summer. The leaves are bright green at first, roughly hairy on both sides, unequal at the base, with large and small teeth. They vary in length from 7 to 15cm.

Wych elm is very tolerant of atmospheric pollution, hence its popularity in Victorian planting schemes for parks. In the uplands it spreads along streams, growing beside alder, and is not found at any altitude, unless well sheltered.

Disease

Dutch elm disease continues to remove elms from the Scottish landscape. The disease has been present in Scotland for as long as elms have, but in the form of the less aggressive species *Ophiostoma ulmi*, which may cause defoliation and die-back in parts of the crown, but rarely leads to the death of a tree. The aggressive form of the disease is caused by the fungus *O. novo-ulmi*, which entered southern Britain in the 1960s.

The aggressive form of this disease travels rapidly through the vascular system, stimulating the production of tyloses by the host tree. These compounds cause blockage of the xylem vessels, followed by the familiar symptoms of yellowing leaves that spread to the whole crown and kill the tree. The key to the disease's mobility is the vector, elm bark beetles of the genus *Scolytus*. They breed by laying their eggs in tunnels under the bark of dying, or recently dead, timber, which has usually been weakened or killed by the action of the fungus. The emerging larvae feed on the cambium and excavate meandering paths radiating outwards from the egg tunnel, later to emerge as adults through holes bored to the outside. The emerging adults carry the spores of *Ophiostoma* and will deposit them on a healthy elm when they fly there to feed, typically in the upper parts of the crown. This creates a fast-moving epidemic to which the elm has little or no resistance. Where trees grow from a single clone of English elm suckers, as they frequently do in hedgerows, only one point of infection is needed to kill a whole community. The identification of an immune strain of English elm so far remains illusory (*see also* page 53).

Where to plant elm

Wych elm will grow on almost any reasonably fertile and well-drained mineral soil. It will stand moderate shade, at least in the early years, and on a good site can grow very vigorously.

The chief factor to be considered when planting is Dutch elm disease. Large groups planted close together will eventually be at risk of root cross-infection, should one become infected by the aerial route. Individual trees, however, may just escape. A few individuals included in new plantings may be all that is required to maintain genetic variation into the future. It is best, then, to gather seed as locally as possible, and plant in ones and twos.

Cultivation

Wych elm should be easy to grow from seed and a usable plant can be obtained in two years. Mature elms typically produce seed every year. It should be collected when the wing begins to turn brown, and before it is dispersed by the wind. In Scotland this is likely to be mid to late June. It should be sown on the same day as it is collected, and well watered both before and after covering with fine grit. Germination takes a few weeks but fertility is low, and viability may be around 40 per cent. It is also possible to store the seed dry, without stratification.

English elm stock is usually found by splitting off young suckers, as seed fertility is very low. This can be done once new sucker growth has become woody.

Uses

The heartwood of elm is rich, reddish-brown, and the sapwood is much lighter. It is usually figured by strong annual rings, making it an attractive wood. It is hard and strong, yet easily worked and not easily split when dry. Its traditional uses were for chair seats, mallet heads, wheel hubs and, famously, for coffins. Burr elm is particularly prized by craftsmen for its complex and attractive grain. Large pieces may be steamed and peeled for veneers, thus commanding very high prices. Smaller burrs may be turned into bowls or used as inlays. The seasoning of elm can be a difficult and wasteful business since elm boards have a tendency to warp horribly. Careful seasoning and storage is important.

Hollowed elm logs were once commonly used as water pipes, and 200-year-old versions of these can be seen in the Museum of Edinburgh. Elm will last almost indefinitely if kept continually wet. It is not particularly durable in contact with soil and air, however, and so does not make good fencing material.

Lore

There is an old Highland belief that an early fall of elm leaves foretells cattle disease the following year. In England the tree has associations with human death, and is considered gloomy, perhaps because it has a reputation for shedding boughs on passers-by, and also because coffins were frequently made with elm boards. An old saying goes 'Elm hateth man, and waiteth'.

Keith Logie
is a Chartered Forester who has spent many years dealing with elms and Dutch elm disease. He works for the City of Edinburgh Council managing greenspace strategy and specialist services.

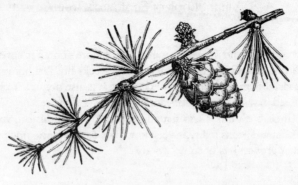

EUROPEAN LARCH
Larix decidua

Although an important timber tree, the deciduous nature of the larch makes it an attractive amenity tree for larger parks and gardens. It is especially lovely just after the first flush of bright green needles, when it also bears its red female cones, and in the autumn when its needles turn golden. This contrast with the evergreen conifers makes the larch a useful tree to bring some diversity into plantation forestry, adding interest to the landscape in reducing the visual monotony that makes coniferous plantations unpopular.

Where it grows

European larch is one of ten species of closely related deciduous conifers found around the Northern Hemisphere in mainly mountainous regions. The native range of the European larch is a broad swathe of upland central Europe, from Switzerland to the mountains of southern Poland. In the Bavarian Alps, larch sometimes forms pure stands, but in the rest of its range it is most commonly found with pines, silver fir, spruce and beech in mixed stands.

What to look for

As a deciduous conifer, larch has needles, but sheds them at the beginning of winter. The first flush of new bright-green needles appears in March. On new shoots the needles grow singly in a spiral pattern, and on old wood they grow in whorls on short spurs.

The female cones appear in March and are a pink colour before turning brown, and the flowers are produced near the end of last year's shoots and are yellow, tinged with pink. The larch has the typical conical conifer shape, with downward-sweeping branches, which arise in whorls. On very old, open grown specimens the lower branches often sweep upwards abruptly about two metres out from the trunk. Growth is fast and larches can reach a height of 18 metres in as many years.

Introduction to Britain

Larch was introduced to the British Isles sometime during the 1620s. John Evelyn, in his first edition of *Silva*, published in 1662, mentions the larch and describes some trees of goodly stature, indicating that they had been growing for some time. He also reveals that its deciduous habit caused much confusion and that his own gardener threw out some carefully raised specimens when their leaves turned yellow in autumn. Nisbet, in his book *British Forest Trees*, published in 1893, states that larch was introduced to England in 1629, into the lowlands of Scotland in 1725 by James Nasmyth of Dawyck, and into the Highlands in 1727 by the Duke of Atholl. Nisbet also states that between 1738 and 1820, 27 million larches were planted in the Highlands. The Duke of Atholl has been credited with making the larch so popular at this time, and great expectations were placed on these plantations. Many of these early plantings used seed of Alpine origin, and although some were successful, a good many suffered from canker and from a condition known as larch dieback. These failures were thought to reflect both site conditions and seed origin.

The Japanese larch, *Larix leptolepis*, was introduced in or around 1861. This closely related species fares better than the European larch in wetter and more elevated conditions and is more resistant to dieback. It is also more accommodating to soil conditions but more susceptible to the effects of drought. It is more tolerant of air pollution and soil contamination and has been used in mine restoration projects. It has strong horizontal branches in contrast to the downward-sweeping branches of the European species.

Hybrids between the two species were first noticed at Dunkeld around 1904, and growth-ring counting revealed that they arose in 1897. This hybrid larch, *Larix x eurolepis,* is also known as the Dunkeld larch and has greater resistance to larch dieback than both the European larch and Japanese larch. First and second-generation hybrids from selected parents have proved successful, but third-generation offspring have been very inferior.

Cultivation

The most desirable silvicultural characteristics for European larch grown in Britain are late flushing of new growth, high growth rate, good stem form, and resistance to canker and dieback. The site requirements for larch are quite exacting: it grows best on moist but well-drained, moderately fertile loams, and should not be planted in areas susceptible to late frosts. Damp hollows, badly drained sites, peats, shallow soils over chalk, and very dry sites should be avoided. Larch has some tolerance of air pollution but does not grow well near exposed coasts.

European larch is a light-demanding pioneer species: it casts only light shade and is a good nurse species for oak, beech and Sitka spruce. Rapid early growth means that thinnings can provide an economic return, and on good sites the rotation can be 40 years. If managed under a continuous-cover system, the light-demanding nature means that silvicultural systems that do not open up relatively large spaces will not work well with larch.

Pests and diseases

Larch canker is caused by the fungus *Lachnellula willkommii.* Susceptibility is related to provenance, with larch from the high Alps being most susceptible to infection and Japanese larch more resistant – as are the hybrids, depending upon parentage. The fungus gains entry around a wound in the bark or through a bud and invades the surrounding live tissue, killing it. If the canker surrounds the trunk, the tree is effectively girdled and dies.

Dieback of larch is caused by infestations of the defoliating insect pest *Adelges laricis,* which often occurs together with canker, and whole plantations can be devastated. As with canker, it is the trees of Alpine origin that are most susceptible to this dieback, while those from the Sudeten region have more resistance. The Japanese and hybrid larches also have more resistance. As with all other conifers used in British forestry, the larches are susceptible to butt rot caused by the fungus *Heterobasidion annosum*.

The recommended provenance today is for seed from Registered British Seed Stands as a first choice, and secondly imported seed from the Sudeten region of the Czech Republic. Seed from high elevations in the Alps should be avoided.

Uses

Larch timber is characterised by a red to brown heartwood and a creamy-brown sapwood. There is a marked distinction between paler springwood and darker summerwood, which makes the annual rings very visible. Larch has a multitude of uses. In the past it was used for high-quality furniture and panelling. Good quality, slow-grown larch is quite hard and has a blunting effect on tools, but can be worked to a fine finish, which takes a good polish. Herring barrels and whisky mash tuns were also made of larch. However, the fast growth of much of the larch currently grown in Britain means that most is not suitable for these uses today.

The heartwood of larch is classed as moderately durable, especially when in contact with the soil or water. Much of the larch grown today is used for fencing, gates, sheds and estate work, and it is increasingly sought after for building work, especially as cladding. Its durability has been recognised for a long time, and many of the piles that support the city of Venice are of larch. Good clear stems of sufficient size are sought by boat builders, as larch makes excellent planking that is very durable in marine conditions. The first boat to be built with larch planking in Britain was a naval frigate, the *Athole*, launched in 1820 at Woolwich. The timber had come from the Duke's estate at Dunkeld. A few years later, a ship was built entirely of Atholl larch in Perth and was appropriately named the *Larch*. Boat builders also used the root buttresses and larger branchwood to make the braces and knees used in boat construction.

The flowers of the larch are used to make one of the Bach flower remedies, this one being used to help people with low self-esteem or who lack confidence. A cold extract of larch bark is used as a diuretic and a laxative and powdered larch bark was used to treat wounds that were difficult to heal.

Turpentine can be obtained by distilling the resin extracted by boring holes in the larch trunk. In addition to its uses in paint making, extracts of turpentine and the unrefined larch balsam are used in throat lozenges.

Lore

In Eastern European folklore the larch was believed to prevent enchantment and to ward off evil spirits. Children were sometimes made to wear collars made of larch bark as a protection against the evil eye.

Douglas Gooday

is a Biologist and furniture maker. He works as an Education Ranger in the North East of Scotland.

Sources

Hart, C., *Practical Forestry for the Agent and Surveyor*. Sutton Publishing, 1991.

Michie, C.Y., *The Larch*. William Blackwood and Sons, 1885.

Nisbet, J., *British Forest Trees*. Macmillan, 1893.

FIELD MAPLE
Acer campestre & Acer species

Although field maple is not a native of Scotland, it appears in lowland hedges and field edges. Its name is thought to derive from the Old German, masa, which also gives 'mazer', a large alms cup traditionally made from maple wood. The field maple has common names such as 'cat oak' or 'whistle-wood' in England but seems to be little noticed in Scotland.

Where to find it

Maples are distributed worldwide, the majority in Asia, but several are native to Europe, notably Norway maple (*Acer platanoides*). This thrives on several Highland estates where it was planted for the sake of its colourful autumn leaves. Others, like the sugar maple (*A. saccharum*) and the red maple (*A. rubrum*), the famous natives of North America, are seldom seen here except in arboretums. Field maple is relatively common as a hedge plant in England and Wales and it is probably as hedging that it has been introduced to Scotland.

What to look for

In hedges field maple will appear as a bushy shrub – one that copes well with trimming, even with flail cutters. Allowed to grow unmolested it can become a sizeable tree. One of the largest in Scotland, at Blairlogie in Stirlingshire, is about 18m tall and said to be three hundred years old. Longish red stalks carry the dark green leaves. Smaller and narrower than the familiar Canadian symbol (*A. rubrum*), the leaves have five neat lobes, only some of which have rounded teeth. In autumn they turn bright yellow rather than flushing red like their North American cousin. Clusters of yellowish flowers emerge with the young leaves in spring, turning to short winged keys, or 'samaras', by early autumn. The light brown bark of the tree is notable for the furrowed, corky appearance that starts to develop when the twigs are a few years old.

Cultivation

Gather the seeds when they are fully ripe, not before October. They are deeply dormant so must be stratified all winter, though this can be done in outside beds if they are protected from predators. They may germinate the first spring but are more likely to do so in the second, or even third one. Seedlings then develop quite rapidly, like those of the sycamore, which they resemble. Field maple is tolerant of shade and can make an interesting addition to a mixed wood where the soil is not too acidic.

Uses and Lore

The wood is fine-grained and good for turning, carving and particularly for making musical instruments, as it has a good sounding quality. The harps found in the Anglo Saxon ship burial at Sutton Hoo were made of field maple. The wood takes a polish well and can be used as a veneer. Field maple is pollution-tolerant and makes an attractive street tree.

The samaras are frequently dubbed 'helicopter blades' by children because their wings are horizontal, rather than drooping (as in the case of the sycamore), and they turn in gyres as they descend to earth.

Fi Martynoga
writes regularly for the Reforesting Scotland Journal and is a long-term member of the Carrifran Wildwood Steering Group.

Sources

Hart, C. & Raymond, C., *British Trees in Colour.* Michael Joseph, 1973.
Mabey, R., *Flora Britannica.* Sinclair-Stevenson, 1996.
Miller, J., *The Trees of the Northern Highlands.* Alness, 1999.

Alder

Ash

Aspen

Beech

Birch

Blackthorn

Bird cherry

Wild cherry

Horse chestnut

Sweet chestnut

Crab apple

Dog rose

Douglas fir

Elder

Elm (*Ulmus glabra*)

European larch

Field maple

Hawthorn

Hazel

Holly

Juniper

Lime

Lodgepole pine

Monkey puzzle

Oak (*Quercus robur*)

Sessile oak (*Quercus petraea*)

Rowan

Scots pine

Sitka spruce

Sycamore

Whitebeam

Willow (*Salix alba*)

Yew

DISEASES: Elongated canker on ash stem

Internal staining of ash wood

Ash dieback

Infected ash foliage

Dutch elm disease

Acute oak decline

Pine pitch canker disease

Pine processionary moth
(*Kiril Sotirovski, FYR Macedonia.*)

Japanese larch with *Phytophthora ramorum* (*Hugh Claydon, FCS*)

Above: Birch trees, Glenlivet; regeneration in Abernethy Forest.

Below: Community-owned woodland in Knoydart.

HAWTHORN
Crataegus monogyna / Sgitheach or Huathe

The Gaelic *sgitheach*, old Gaelic *huathe* or *uath*, was considered to be feminine, a queen amongst trees. The current Gaelic name appears in a few place names, such as Loch Sgitheeach on Jura, Loch Skiach in Perthshire and Abhain Sgitheach in Easter Ross, but the old name does not seem to be remembered in this way.

Where it grows

The hawthorn is of the family *Rosaceae*, and genus *Crataegus*. Of some two hundred worldwide, only two are native to Britain. *Crataegus oxyanthus*, the Midland hawthorn, is now localised in central and south-east England, while *Crataegus monogyna* is common throughout England, eastern and southern Scotland, and present in the Highlands and islands. In the past, however, the former would have been more widespread, it being adapted to conditions within woodland. The latter is a ready coloniser and typically a tree of clearings and the woodland edge.

The use of hawthorn for hedging is documented as far back as 1316, and is shown by the archaeological record to be even more ancient. At Barr Hill on the Antonine Wall, excavators found hawthorn branches with characteristic marks of hedge laying underneath the Roman fort, taking hawthorn hedges back to before 146 AD. Although this early cultivation of the plant complicates the picture of its distribution, hawthorn is almost certainly native throughout Scotland and can still be found growing wild in most areas.

What to look for

Hawthorn generally takes the form of a shrub, or a small tree if it is allowed to grow unchecked. It rarely grows to more than 5m in a hedge but can attain 9m in tree form and lives up to 300 years, which is exceptional in a tree of such stature. One ancient example at Hethel, near Norwich, is estimated by the Norfolk Wildlife Trust to be 700 years old and has a girth of 4.26 metres!

Hawthorns typically display numerous strong branches supporting a dense network of thin, dark twigs with pink buds. Many of these develop into sharp thorns – a godsend to farmers in need of stock-proof fencing, even today. Buds burst early in spring, reliably, even after harsh winters, and the three-to-seven-lobed leaves give early nourishment for animals. The five-petalled flowers appear shortly afterwards, heralding the summer. They range from white to deep pink in common hawthorn; the flowers of the Midland thorn are larger and exclusively white. These flowers are fertilised principally by carrion insects, which are attracted to their smell of decomposition. The Glastonbury thorn, which flowers twice, appears to be a common hawthorn grafted on to a blackthorn stock. The berries or haws are oval, red and single-stoned, or two-to-three-stoned in the case of the Midland thorn.

The hawthorn supports a greater number of invertebrate species than other hedging shrubs, and the haws stay on the trees to offer winter food to a wide variety of birds. The traditional name 'white thorn' implies a contrast with the sloe of blackthorn. The pale bark of young hawthorn twigs darkens and fissures with age into a jigsaw of squares and rectangles on the sturdy and often twisted, gnarled trunk.

Cultivation

Hawthorn, also known as 'May tree', 'quick thorn' or 'quickset', combines rapid, sturdy growth with an ability to flourish in virtually any situation. It is shade-tolerant (the Midland thorn more so) and can survive on acidic soils and in windy sites, although it will struggle in more extreme, particularly maritime, conditions, where blackthorn is the more appropriate choice. The Midland thorn is less robust.

Early hedge-layers tended to gather seedlings from the wild and grew some plants from cuttings, but as the plant grows so well from seed, this is the preferred method. The berries may be collected from October onwards and stratified in sand for two winter seasons in order to break dormancy. Alternatively, they may be allowed to rot, the flesh removed, and the seed stored in well-drained sand for one winter only. Sown in seed-beds in the spring, plants may be large enough to transplant after one growing season. Leave the seedbed as there may be some secondary germination the following year. Plants are vulnerable to browsing in formative years but are resilient once established.

When used for hedging, plants may be set in single rows, spaced at about 23cm or in double rows 15cm apart, at 25cm spacing, or even in three rows to increase windbreak effects and inpenetrability. To maximise wildlife value where stock-proofing is not a priority, a mixed hedge is recommended. Combine about 50 per cent thorn with such species as field maple, blackthorn, dogwood, wayfaring tree, buckthorn, guelder rose, goat willow, hazel, crab apple and bird cherry, depending on conditions. The thorn provides protection for the slower-growing and more vulnerable species, and the combination offers an all-year habitat that will give food and shelter for nesting birds.

A hawthorn hedge can be layered every 10 to 15 years to keep it impenetrable, or simply trimmed to maintain its form. However, it does not coppice well and may die if cut back too severely. A further word of warning is that hawthorn is susceptible to fire blight bacteria and so may be inappropriate to plant in the vicinity of fruit trees. It is also host to the carrot-hawthorn aphid, which may be worth noting.

Uses

The many names of this plant reflect its myriad uses. 'Quickthorn' probably refers not only to its rapid growth as a hedge but to 'quick', meaning living, as people in the past would use brushwood for 'dead-hedges' and hawthorn for living ones. The vigorous rootstock may be used for grafting medlar and pear varieties as well as members of its own species. The Latin name stems from the Greek *kratos,* meaning hardness, and refers to the wood, particularly the root wood, which was used for boxes and combs.

The timber is prized for turning small items, carvings, utensils, and tool handles, as well as providing excellent fuelwood, especially for charcoal. The names 'lady's meat' and 'bread and butter tree' reflect the edibility of the young leaves. The berries are also palatable in the form of jelly, or turned into wine or vinegar. Teas may be prepared from the flowers, leaves or berries. They are valued medicinally for cardiac, diuretic, astringent and tonic properties and are useful for sore throats, hypertension, heart, and kidney problems.

Lore

Long connected with femininity, the hawthorn's life-cycle was taken as symbolic of the transition of the seasons and, in parallel, the patterns of maturation within the life of a woman.

'May' blossoms, heralding the birth of summer, were essential adornment for the maypole and, in associated ceremonies, for the May Queen herself. There are tales in the Highlands of ritual worship of the spring goddess in sacred enclosures of hawthorn, to ensure the safe transition of the season. The cuckoo is also associated with the thorn in myth, as is the Elfin Queen in a number of folk tales.

Hawthorn's magic touch, however, was not always benevolent. In some regions of Scotland an association with the hereditary chiefs meant that any demise of the trees would be ominous for the line. In many areas it was considered too great an affront to the forces of evil to bring hawthorn into the home. She was the ultimate symbol of the sacred, untouchable, wild. Further, an association with death seems to have stemmed from the heavy, slightly fetid perfume of the flowers, and the tree's readiness to colonise deserted hamlets after the Black Death. In England, the Old English word for hedge, *haga* (pronounced 'haw'), reflects the inextricable link between the thorn's folklore and its supreme value as a barrier to separate 'horn from corn'. This gives the plant a long association with enclosure, waves of which have swept through Britain from mediaeval times.

Jacqui Yelland

HAZEL
Corylus avellana / Col, or Caltuinn

Of all the trees that have a significant place in Celtic lore (and pre-Celtic, pan-Celtic and sub-Celtic) some six to nine species stand out, and hazel is certainly one of these. Its early presence, its wide geographical spread and density, and the abundance of its values to the environment and to people all contribute to its high ranking in the hierarchy of sacred plants. Bounteous and hardy, it has been used and venerated by peasants, priests and heroes for thousands of years, exploited and celebrated without taboo but with layers of ritual and symbolism.

Where it grows
Corylus avellana is the only hazel native to Scotland, and there are no sub-species. The name *Corylus* is akin to ancient Gaelic *coll* and modern Gaelic *caltuinn*. Coll gives its name to the island in Argyll and to Clan McColl; *caltuinn* is seen in Barcaldine on the Argyll mainland and Calton Hill in Edinburgh. Hazel is rare in the mountainous and acidic interior, where pine, birch and juniper dominate, but in other parts, birch is a common companion of hazel, as are oak and ash. Its favoured habitats are mostly in the West Highlands, and the fertile straths of the east and south-east, including Fife, and the marginal lands of the south-west. Hazel is rarer in the Southern Uplands but this is largely a result of the heavy grazing of the hills, and the tidying and policy-planting of the valleys.

However, it can safely be said that the hazel tree is native to every county in Scotland. Clusters and individuals can be found huddling in crevices and gullies on tiny islands of the furthest west and north, and it is naturally an inhabitant of the rich farmlands of the east and south. It was an early coloniser of the semi-tundra landscape about 10,000 years ago. It is hardy and virile, and acts as a nursery plant to greater trees and even to lesser plants. Not so many centuries ago there were great sweeps of hazel in the Orkneys, Shetland and the Outer Hebrides. Their established presence contributed significantly to the early development of a rich human culture in these places, both through their enriching of the soil and through their bounteous products. On some far-flung promontories – for example, the Ross of Mull – close woodlands of almost pure hazel represent the uninterrupted succession from those prehistoric woods where Neolithic families settled and worked.

What to look for

With a maximum height of about 10.5m, and usually much less than this, the hazel is a small tree, and because of its natural tendency to have a crooked and leaning trunk, with vigorous roots from root and trunk, it is often termed a shrub. The fact that the majority of specimens have been coppiced in the past further increases their shrubby appearance: when the main stem is cut it encourages a profusion of straight stems. These can be harvested in their turn, which increases the life expectancy of the tree (unless it is already very mature) from about 200 to 300–400 years. The downside of coppicing is that it interrupts, or even curtails, an individual tree's power of reproduction. However, uncoppiced or rarely coppiced hazel trees will regularly produce an abundance of ripe nuts in October or November. The familiar long, greenish-yellow male catkins of the late winter shed golden pollen, which is carried by the wind to fertilise the small, red, female catkins, here and there on neighbouring twigs or neighbouring trees. The fertilised female flowers swell into the nuts, which form in clusters of two or three.

The leaf buds open in April, and in some years the large, roundish leaves – turning yellow or orange – are still on the trees in early December.

The main trunk, or trunks, and mature branches and shoots, are commonly covered with a patchwork of mosses, lichens and liverworts, particularly in the mild, wet climate of the west coast where the air is relatively clean. This feature makes it difficult to describe the colouring and texture of the bark, but it is usually a shiny grey-brown, darker towards the branch tips.

Where to plant

Hazel will grow anywhere where the soil is not too acidic, and where low, bushy ground cover or under-storey is required. It can be the main component of a woodland or be planted with oak or ash, or with smaller decorative trees such as rowan and cherry. It will do particularly well if planted with oak leaf-mould and where the topography and climate allow for a balance of good damp ground and good drainage. Staking and tree-shelter planting are not ideal as they inhibit the tree's ability to bush.

Cultivation

Collect ripe nuts in October and November. Put them into water and discard those that float. A further soaking of up to two days can increase the germination rate. Either sow immediately into slightly acidic soil or compost, or stratify over winter in leaf-mould and sow in spring. The latter method is advisable where there is a problem with mice. Sow at a depth of about 2.5cm and 2.5cm apart. These same measurements apply if the nuts are sown in a seed tray. Germination should be fast, and within a few weeks seedlings can be spaced out at 30–45cm, or potted.

Uses

It is hard to put this huge topic in a nutshell! The timber itself is not of enormous value but is suitable for certain items of carving and turning, is quite good as fuel, and very good for charcoal. The straighter stems and coppice growth have a wide variety of applications. Thin stems are used for basketry, including fishing creels, and for pea and bean poles; tradition-ally they were used as switches for driving cattle, to protect them against sickness. Thicker stems are used for thatch sup-ports, for walking sticks and shepherds' crooks, and for hurdles – the woven fence sections once so widely used. Leaves have been used in dyeing and as a foodstuff for cows to increase their milk yield. The nuts can be eaten as they are, or dried and ground and mixed with flour. It is recorded that the garrison of Robert Bruce's castle on Loch Fyne was detailed to gather great quantities of hazelnuts to supplement their winter diet. In the past, hazelnuts were rubbed on furniture, where their oils imparted a polish and acted as a preservative.

Lore

In the ancient traditions of Scotland and Ireland the hazel's greatest role has been as a marker or companion of the sacred well of life itself. Nine hazel trees surround the pool, dropping nuts of wisdom into its pure, clear water. There they are eaten by the sacred salmon, or float down the streams that issue from the well to be eaten by a salmon further downstream or in the sea. The nuts, either consumed directly or via the salmon that is eaten by priest or hero, impart wisdom, enlightenment or the revelation of personal fate to whoever consumes them.

This story, reflecting the central importance of hazel as a resource, has long been an important theme in the oral and written mythology of the Celtic lands. However, it was not brought by Celtic incomers, but inherited from the earlier inhabitants.

In the Celtic era the tree has had long associations with the predominantly druidic priesthood, but in tradition the sacred hazel well is cared for and frequented by female priests as representatives of the Mother Goddess. An earlier female priesthood may have been supplanted by male druidism, yet the significance of the hazel continued. Druids and seers are said to have made predictions of great import by watching the direction in which hazelnuts jumped when dropped into a fire. More humbly, a hazelnut placed under the pillow at

Hallowe'en was believed to induce the sleeper to see a spouse-to-be in their dreams. Thus it has had a place both in cosmology and in everyday life, from the divining rod in the hands of megalithic geomancers to the priestesses gazing at the branch reflections in the moonlit pool, from the wand in the hand of the druid to the Hallowe'en dreams of the girl looking for her beloved, or from the fence protecting food crops to the stick an old man uses to help him get about.

Hugh Fife

is a long-standing member of Reforesting Scotland and one of the main instigators of the Blarbuie Woodland Project in Argyll, which he co-ordinates.

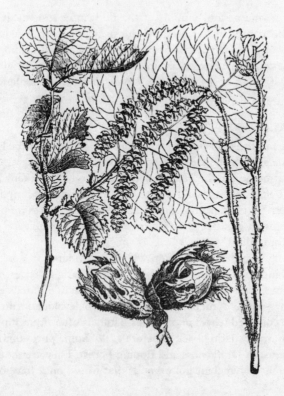

HOLLY
Ilex aquifolium / Chuilinn

Holly is one of the symbols of the midwinter festival. It has long been used in decorations during winter, its lush green foliage and red berries bringing freshness and colour into the darkness. Holly is not a common tree in Scotland, but all the same, it is an easily recognised part of native woodland in many parts of the country.

Where it grows

Of the family *Aquifoliaceae*, holly, *Ilex aquifolium*, is in the large genus *Ilex*, which has 400 species worldwide. *Ilex* was the Roman name for the Holm Oak, which holly was likened to, holm being one of its old names. In 1753 Linnaeus simplified a system for classification and used the genus *Quercus* for oaks, so the holm oak became *Quercus ilex*, and the genus *Ilex* was used for hollies.

Holly most commonly grows in the under-storey of oak woodland, but is often found in other woodland types. It is also found on rocky hillsides up to an altitude of 550m. Widely grown in gardens, many varieties have been developed with different coloured leaves and berries. Holly is often found in old hedges, many dating back to before 1700. Some pure stands of holly exist in Dungeness and Epping Forest. They are thought to be relics of ancient holly woods that would once have been widespread in England, Scotland and Ireland. These stands are of particularly high conservation value, as holly woods are thought to have been unique to Britain.

What to look for

Holly generally takes the form of a small tree, although, given light and space, it can grow up to 23m tall. In dense woodland the trunk usually divides near to the ground, becoming twisted and irregular. The branches grow in an untidy tangle: they are long and narrow, hanging down to the ground (where they sometimes root) and curling up at the ends. The bark is almost always grey and smooth.

Holly is one of our few evergreen broadleaves. The tough, shiny leaves are full of oils, preventing water loss, and are highly flammable. They are one of the few food sources available in winter, so the lower leaves develop sharp, protective spines. Each leaf lives for two to three years and is usually shed in spring.

Holly first flowers at age 20. The flowers are grouped near to the base of the leaves and are pale purple until they open in May, when they become white. They are pretty and fragrant but short-lived. Most are either male or female, so must be pollinated by flying insects, usually bees. This explains why lone specimens often remain barren. By Christmas the ovaries of the female flowers have ripened to become the familiar scarlet berries, which are produced in greatest profusion during mast years when the tree is over 40 years old.

Cultivation

Holly grows well in most conditions, especially in the milder south and west. It flourishes in acidic soils, but avoids wet conditions. It can tolerate deep shade and also casts it, which prevents most species from flourishing beneath it. It tolerates pollution and is often planted in towns for this reason. Holly berries do not go bad or fall off the tree, even when frosted, and can last through the winter, unless they are eaten by birds, which will then scatter the indigestible seeds. Germination never takes place in the first year, so berries need to be stratified in sand for two winters to rot off the flesh and weaken the hard seed-coat. There are usually about 4500 seeds per 100g, 80 per cent of which will normally germinate. Holly is very sensitive to transplanting, which must be done with great care during the growing season (approximately May to September).

Uses

Holly is slow-growing, which results in white wood that is hard, dense and heavy, without any distinct heartwood or sapwood. The grain is very fine and even but can distort whilst the wood is drying. It stains and polishes well, making it prized for decorative furniture. Wood turners use holly for small items, bowls and chess pieces. Its hardness makes it useful for tool handles and, reputedly, for chariot shafts! The timber also makes excellent firewood that burns well even when green. The holly tree used to be coppiced or pollarded for winter fodder for sheep and deer. You can still see veterans that bear the scars of frequent cutting for this purpose. The bark was boiled to make birdlime for trapping small birds. Boiled young leaves were recommended as a cure for colds, bronchitis and rheumatism. Its prickly leaves make holly useful as a hedge plant, and it has been found to be an effective nurse for some young tree seedlings.

Lore

In Gaelic lore the *chuilinn* had protective power, warding off evil spirits. In England it was planted to ward off witches and lightning, and to repel poison. It is sometimes found in churchyards. Even today, some consider it unlucky to cut down a holly, particularly in Ireland, where it is a home for fairies. For the Romans, holly was a symbol of peace and goodwill, and this symbolism was carried over in the holly Christmas decorations of Christians. Holly also represents Christ, the spiky leaves signifying the crown of thorns, and the red berries the blood, as the old carol tells us.

Rebecca Mitchell

trained in Ecology and Forestry. She worked for some time with Reforesting Scotland, and for other forestry projects in Scotland. She now devotes her time to her family and to a school near Cambridge, which offers 'education in the woods'.

JUNIPER
Juniperus communis / Aittin, or samh

Few people would immediately list juniper as native to Scotland, as they more often associate it with hotter, drier climates. It is, however, ancient, being one of the first pioneers to arrive in northern Britain shortly after the last ice age, 10,000 or more years ago. It is also one of Britain's most threatened species and is now part of the UK Biodiversity Action Plan. Scottish clans have long used plants as 'badges' to form part of their cultural identification, and Clan Brodie is linked to juniper, along with Ross, Murray and Gunn. The Gaelic names for juniper, *aittin* and *samh* can be seen in a few place names, such as Attadale in Wester Ross, and Samhan, an island close to Mull. *Samh* is associated with Samhain, or Hallowe'en, as juniper was burnt at the entrances of Scottish homes to keep away evil spirits on that night.

Where it grows

There are about sixty species of *Juniperus* worldwide, from Canada to the Mediterranean to Japan, but *J. communis* is one of only three conifers native to Britain, the other two being yew and Scots pine. A member of the *Cupressaceae* family, it is a gymnosperm, meaning naked-seeded. Its ovule, or unfertilised seed, lies exposed on a cone scale. Once fertilised, the cone scale becomes fleshy and forms a galbulus (often mistakenly called a berry) around the seed, holding it until it ripens. In this respect it resembles yew rather than other conifers, and in Scotland the juniper is often called the mountain yew.

In Britain juniper can be found as far north as Orkney, with small stands in the Lake District, the Scottish Borders, and the Western Isles. But today it is common only in two main districts, the central Highlands of Scotland and the chalk hills of southern England. These two habitats could hardly be more different.

In the north, juniper prefers wet, peaty, acidic hillsides, growing with heather on moorland and in the under-storey of the old Highland birch and pine woods. It can be seen in abundance in the Rothiemurchus Forest, Inverness-shire, and some of the finest examples of dwarf juniper scrub can be found on the north slopes of Beinn Eighe in Wester Ross. One of the largest remaining stands is the five-hectare Tynron Juniper Wood, near Thornhill in Dumfriesshire.

In southern Britain juniper grows on the hot, dry, calcium-rich soils of the lowland chalk country, especially in the Chilterns. Further south in Wiltshire, a bizarre setting for the largest population in England is within the high-security fencing of the Ministry of Defence's Porton Down establishment (known for chemical and biological research). The overall security probably explains why more than 14,000 bushes grow here with little disturbance. Bushes can also be seen on road embankments in this county.

What to look for

Juniper is usually a low shrub but can grow as a tree up to 3m, and in exceptional circumstances, up to 10m high. The shape varies with the location and climate. In the south junipers are sometimes spreading or conical trees. In the north they grow as small shrubs on the lower slopes of the Highlands, and at greater altitude, as prostrate shrubs. Juniper is very slow-growing, adding only a few centimetres a year, but has a life of 70 years or more. Older trees have a tendency to die out from the centre and collapse. This can be seen in one of the most long-standing populations in Britain, on the Taynish peninsula in Argyll, where there are almost no young bushes.

Resembling gorse, juniper is easily recognised by its aromatic foliage of sharp-pointed needles set along the branches in groups of three. When crushed a sharp smell of gin is given off. The needles are blue-green, with a white, waxy covering. Unlike many tree species, juniper is dioecious (each tree is either male or female), and where there are low numbers of juniper, this noticeably restricts the amount of regeneration. The male flowers open in spring as bunches of yellow blossom near the twig tips, and release pollen. Female flowers are very small and bud-like, no more than a cluster of open scales, and are pollinated by insects or the wind. These scales have developed into round, green berries by the autumn, but it takes several more months for them to ripen into black fruits in their second year.

Cultivation

Juniper is able to reproduce from about seven years of age, although it is notoriously slow to grow from seed. The berries usually contain three to six hard, black, triangular seeds. Unlike other seeds, juniper can be gathered all year. Flowers, unripe green berries and ripe blue ones can all be found on the plants at the same time. The berries should be stratified in moist sand for about 18 months before they can be sown. Germination then takes place over a further 18 months, some seedlings emerging soon, and others much later. When they sprout, they raise two slender seed leaves, followed by the typical spiky needles.

An alternative way of propagating juniper is to take side cuttings between August and October and plant them out in a cold frame. Tip-cuttings are also possible, and Borders Forest Trust has had success with this method. In the wild, birds help with the spread and germination of juniper seed. Fire also contributes to the plant's regeneration, for it is hardy enough to withstand blazes, as well as snow, intense cold, and wind. Grazing animals, however, are a hazard, and growth will be restricted unless plants are protected from herbivores.

Uses

The best-known product from juniper is oil from the berries, which is used to flavour gin. European law requires that these aromatic berries be the predominant ingredient of distilled gin, providing it with its distinctive flavour. Native juniper went out of use with British distillers in the 19th century but has recently been revived by some smaller companies. In the past surplus berries were shipped from the markets of Aberdeen and Inverness to Holland, the home of gin. Most juniper berries are now imported from Italy and Eastern Europe.

Juniper wood is of little use for furniture or building, but its trunk, with reddish bark, pinkish-brown heartwood, and white sapwood, is attractive for ornamental carving or tool handles. In Sutherland, babies were given teething twigs of juniper, which were also claimed to provide protection against harm.

The berries can be used to spice soups and stews, particularly of venison or other game, but they are also good in vegetable soups or even in salads. Ground berries can be used to add a tang to cakes and breads. As firewood, juniper burns freely because of its resinous oil and produces a cedar-like fragrance that is added to give flavour when smoking hams and cheeses. However, juniper produces almost no visible smoke, and one of the reasons given for juniper being less common than it was in earlier times is that it was cut for burning in illicit whisky stills, so that their fires would give the excise men no clues.

To increase woodland biodiversity, juniper is often recommended for planting when new native pinewoods are being established. As a shrub in some Scottish native pine and birch woods, juniper provides nesting cover for birds such as thrush and goldcrest. Although it is not a favourite food for many birds, migratory fieldfares and waxwings from Scandinavia relish the berries in winter. The German name for fieldfare is *Wacholderdrossel*, or juniper thrush. Juniper is a food source for the caterpillars of the small juniper pug (*Eupithecia pusillata*) and the attractive juniper carpet moths (*Thera juniperata*).

Medicinally, juniper has been in use since Roman times as a cure for stomach complaints, epilepsy, and even snakebites. Juniper wood was burnt in homes to fumigate against infectious diseases. The berries also have a strong diuretic effect. Juniper should be avoided during pregnancy as it can cause serious complications. The essential oil of juniper is now used therapeutically in aromatherapy to ease arthritis, respiratory infections, eczema and oily skin conditions.

Occasionally, juniper is infected by a gall-midge (*Oligotrophus juniperinus*), which produces a gall-like swelling on its stem. This is known as the whooping-cough gall, because of the medicinal uses to which it has been put.

Shrubs propagated in the 1990s are now doing well at several sites in the Scottish Borders and elsewhere. We can safely say that this particular native is being welcomed back to parts (areas) of Scotland's landscape that have lacked it for generations.

Sam Murray,

a former Information Officer of Reforesting Scotland, is now a gardener who campaigns enthusiastically for allotments.

Sources

Borders Forest Trust & University of Edinburgh, Common Juniper, (Juniperus communis L.): a review of biology and status in the Scottish Borders. Occasional Paper No. 1, Borders Forest Trust, Jedburgh, 1997.

Fife, H. *Warriors and Guardians: Native Highland Trees.* Argyll, 1994

Mabey, R., *Flora Britannica.* Sinclair-Stevenson, 1996

Managing uplands for Juniper, Back from the Brink Management Series, Plantlife International, Salisbury, 2005: http://www.plantlife.org.uk/uploads/documents/Management-Managing-uplands-for-juniper.pdf

Broome, A., *Growing juniper: propagation and establishment practices.* Forestry Commission Information Note FCIN50, 2003: http://www.forestry.gov.uk/pdf/FCIN050.pdf/$FILE/FCIN050.pdf

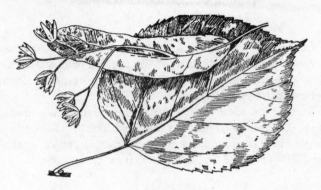

LIME
Tilia spp.

The Old English name for lime was *lind*, which occurs as the element 'lin' in many English place names. However, do not be misled by that element in Scots place names! Where it occurs it most often means waterfall, from the Gaelic *linn*, or occasionally may refer to the flax used for linen making, from the Latin *linum*. The reason for the lack of lime place names is, as you will see, an absence of the tree from Scotland in earlier times.

Lime trees, which constitute the genus *Tilia*, are easily recognised: all are deciduous and have soft, often heart-shaped leaves which are mucilaginous (that is, the leaves are palatable but slimy when chewed). What, however, marks a lime uniquely is the presence of pale green, paddle-shaped bracts, from the middle of which branch bouquets of small, cream-coloured, sweetly scented flowers.

Worldwide well over a hundred limes have been described. In fact, there are probably not more than 24, which are all found in the woodlands of the northern temperate zone in America, Asia and Europe. Two species are native in western Europe: the small-leaved lime, *Tilia cordata* (Fig. 1) and the large-leaved lime, *T. platyphyllos* (Fig. 2).

Much of the confusion over *Tilia* species has arisen from a failure to appreciate both the extent of genetic variation within populations and the developmental variation within a single tree. This second source of variation is important for identification because it is the leaves on the well-lit flowering shoots, as well as the bracts, flowers and fruits, which differ between species. Leaves on the shaded lower branches, on the sprouts which arise from coppicing and on young trees are very different and much more uniform between species. Unfortunately, it is lower shoots that are accessible and, in woodland, flowering shoots are 20–30m above the ground. This is a familiar problem to those who have worked in tropical forests.

Hybrids

Problems also arise from the existence of hybrids, both natural, where two species grow mixed together, and in cultivation, because some have been propagated in nurseries, especially in the Netherlands and England, and extensively planted. The hybrid between *T. cordata* and *T. platyphyllos* is the common lime (*T. x europaea*), of which some clones are fertile, and consequently trees with almost all combinations of characteristics have arisen and some closely resemble *T. platyphyllos*. A few hybrid clones have been propagated vegetatively on a large scale and planted in towns and parks, often for avenues. Within each clone the trees are uniform and quite distinct, so that understandably they were often regarded as distinct species. For example, a widely planted clone, known in Germany as Kaiserlinde, was described by Frederick Hayne as *T. vulgaris* but, if its seedlings are raised, the trees show an extraordinary range of genetic variation (including dwarf varieties) and are clearly the progeny of a hybrid. A large tree of this clone, still very much alive in Uppsala in Sweden, is probably the source of the type specimen of *T. europaea* in the herbarium of Linnaeus, and so this distinctive variety must by the rules be called *T. europaea var. europaea*. It is not uncommonly planted in Scotland and often misidentified as *T. cordata*. The fluted trunk, often disfigured by lumpy masses of dormant buds or sprouts, the hanging, narrow, elliptical bracts and inflorescences, usually of seven flowers, make the variety easily recognisable.

In my experience hybrids are the cause of many difficulties in identification because they are so common, and flowering shoots of trees planted in the open are more accessible than those of the parent species when growing in woods. Also, leaves on the shaded lower shoots of *T. cordata* are very like those of *T.x europaea*. With flowering or fruiting shoots there truly are no problems. The most important characteristics are more easily illustrated than described (see Figs 1 & 2 on pages 167 and 168).

Where are limes native?

The planting of limes has, to some extent, made it difficult to be certain where they are native. In England and Wales, hybrids and *T. platyphyllos* are the most often planted, but in Scotland, for example in Glasgow, *T.cordata* was a popular choice in the twentieth century. Although *T. cordata* was regarded as native in England by Philip Miller when he named the species in 1765, doubts about the status of *T. platyphyllos* have been expressed as recently as 1987 in *Flora of the British Isles*[1]. The preservation of pollen, and occasionally of fruits, in peats and sediments dating back to prehistoric times shows convincingly that both species are native to England and Wales but, as I shall show, probably not to Scotland.

History and evidence of status

Lime pollen is readily identified and, unusually within a genus, that of the two species can also be separated. The flowers are insect-pollinated and the pollen grains tend to stick together, so that, unlike wind-pollinated trees, the pollen is not widely dispersed and most is washed by rain from the trees or falls to the ground within 100m of its source. Consequently anything more than a single isolated grain in a sample of peat indicates the presence of trees close by at the time of deposition. For example, pollen of both species of lime was found by Dorothy Trotman[2] in peat of the bog at the foot of the limestone cliff of Craig y Cilau, near Brecon. Although plentiful in the lower layers, which were formed 6000 to 4000 years ago, it also occurs sparsely up to the present surface, showing that the lime trees on the cliff above are surely native.

The same technique has been successfully applied by Winifred Pennington (unpublished) to peat deposits in small hollows in woodland in the English Lake District. Analyses show that *T. cordata* was common in the southern valleys until 5000 to 2500 years ago but then decreased and, in woods where there is now no lime, its pollen is absent from the upper layers. In contrast, where large ancient limes are still present in the narrow rocky trenches of the fellside becks, lime pollen continues up to the surface. This shows that the limes are direct descendants of those in the prehistoric woodlands and that these narrow strips are much changed fragments of those woods. The oak woods on the intervening slopes occupy land which was cleared and grazed from the Norse settlement to the end of the Middle Ages, a period marked by a layer with abundant grass pollen and bracken spores.

Distribution

Pollen analyses are available from many sites scattered over northern England and southern Scotland. If maximum values for lime pollen (as a percentage of all tree pollen) are plotted on a map (Fig 3, page 160), there is a significant difference between those sites to the north and to the south of the Scottish border. All sites with values above 1 per cent lie to the south and all sites to the north contain only isolated grains. However, because dispersal of lime pollen is so limited, isolated localities of small-leaved lime in the Southern Uplands may have existed but too far away to be recorded in any of the sites from which pollen analyses are available.

In spite of this evidence, the *New Atlas of the British and Irish Flora* (Preston, Pearman & Dines 2002) shows all records for Scotland and Ireland as native. I have discussed this (Pigott 2003) and appealed for specimens from probable native sites, but none has been forthcoming since then.

Natural regeneration

In southern England both native species of lime set fertile seed and, if parent trees are numerous and conditions in the wood are favourable, there can be seedlings, saplings and eventually young trees all present. *Tilia cordata* behaves like beech: small quantities of seeds produce low densities of seedlings, which rarely result in regeneration because predation by wood mice and bank voles destroys the crop. Successful regeneration follows years when there were large crops of seeds, giving rise to high densities of seedlings, which may also have coincided with low predator numbers.

In north-western England, there is sparse regeneration in woods around the coast of Morecambe Bay but none inland in the valleys of the southern Lake District. In the hills, temperatures at flowering time in July and early August are lower than along the sunnier, sheltered parts of the coast and normally just too low (by about 2°C) to allow fertilisation of the ovules and their subsequent development. As a result, a majority of fruits contain no seeds. Only in summers which are abnormally warm, such as 1976 and 1983, are sufficient fertile seeds produced to give a few seedlings under the trees, but in almost all localities the parent trees tend to be isolated or scattered along the rocky banks of becks (burns). As in southern England, sparse seedlings are soon lost to predators.

Inevitably these northern populations consist of old trees, many of them with a number of stems arising from enormous stools, or rings of stools, up to as much as 10 metres in diameter. There is evidence that these are likely to be several centuries old. In fact, regrowth from stools and fallen stems seems to give lime trees near immortality. Almost certainly if there were native localities in the Southern Uplands of Scotland, they would consist of similar trees in the same kind of habitat.

Remarkably, although having a natural northern limit further south, on the limestone cliffs of Swaledale in Yorkshire, *T. platyphyllos* has a lower temperature threshold for fertilisation, and even in Scotland planted trees produce such large quantities of fertile seeds that seedlings and saplings sometimes appear under solitary individuals.

Native lime as an indicator of ancient woodland

The combination of exceptional longevity of individual trees and failure to regenerate from seeds means that trees can 'hang on' almost indefinitely in old woodlands but are unable to colonise new ones. In the nineteenth century, Charles Babington in his *Manual of British Botany*[3] wrote perceptively that *T. cordata* occurs in 'old woods'. Many recent surveys have confirmed this useful attribute, so that to discover this handsome tree in a wood is particularly rewarding because of its historical significance. Planting of the species in apparently natural situations destroys this 'specialness' (champagne should not be drunk every day!) and has an effect not unlike scattering prehistoric artefacts.

Planting young trees will also confuse what is essentially a large-scale natural experiment. Wild populations of *T. cordata* near their northern limit should be very sensitive to global warming, and we would expect a relatively small rise in temperatures to cause not only earlier flowering (which seems to be happening), but also greater frequency of large crops of fertile seeds. Will this allow regeneration and spread to new sites or have woods become unfavourable in other ways? We have a lot to learn from accurate observation of future events.

Lastly, many lime trees supplied by nurseries as *T.cordata* are either of foreign provenance or have evidence of hybridity and these may respond differently from native trees.

Cultivation

So, if you want to plant limes, and for beekeepers *T. platyphyllos* makes good sense, then all I ask is avoid putting them in situations where they will masquerade as natives. Large gardens, parks, avenues and urban woodlands are appropriate places but, because in towns lime-aphids often infest trees and drop sticky honey-dew, they are not popular in car parks!

All limes grow well on deep, moist, but not wet, soils. *Tilia cordata* is at home on deep loams and clays, even those which are poorly aerated, but not waterlogged. *T. platyphyllos* is usually native in Britain on soils over limestone or basic volcanic rocks but, in fact, both species have a wide tolerance of soil conditions. Adult trees are deeply rooted and will tolerate exposure, but the leaves often wind-scorch. Both species will persist in deep shade for at least 20 to 30 years but strong upward growth awaits a gap in the canopy. The leading shoot of a four-to-five-year-old sapling may then grow 0.6 to 1.0m a year. In woods, flowering does not start until a well-grown tree is at least 25 to 35 years old.

It is the small fruits of limes that are collected and sown. As already explained, many fruits of *T. cordata* may be seedless but, when fertile, contain one seed (more rarely, two). Fruits should be stratified soon after collection and exposed to outside winter temperatures (0 to 5°C). Up to 10 per cent may germinate in the first spring and the remainder one to three years later. Both seeds and seedlings must be protected from mice, voles and the small grey garden slugs.

After one year, seedlings are best lined out in a nursery for four to five years before planting out. They soon develop mycorrhiza but still respond to small additions of fertiliser. Propagation from stump sprouts and layering was used traditionally, but most nursery stock is chip-budded. Propagation by cuttings using the current year's growth, taken in July or August and placed in mist, is usually successful.

Uses

Colloquial names for lime trees in many languages refer directly or indirectly to its fibrous, inner bark, known in English as 'bast' or 'bass'. This was widely used from prehistoric times to the start of the last century for making rope, bindings, string, nets, fabric, and even sandal-like shoes. To supply bast, lime was grown as coppice to give unbranched poles, from which bark was peeled and 'retted' to free the fibrous strands. No doubt the wood was used as fuel but it burns quickly and has a low calorific value.

The soft but relatively strong timber has a uniform texture, allowing it to be cut in all directions. It was used by prehistoric people to make dug-out canoes and planks for larger boats, but is ideal for wood carving. Grinling Gibbons executed his intricate designs of flowers, foliage and creatures in this beautiful material.

Young lime leaves are palatable and can be added to spring salads. The taste is good but some may not like the slimy texture. Lime flowers dry easily and make a delicious tea. Pick them on a warm day when the bees are on them and they will be sweet and fragrant. Honey, of course, is another, indirect but excellent, product of lime flowers.

Donald Pigott

researched and taught experimental plant ecology at several British universities, ending his career as Director of the University Botanic Garden, Cambridge. His interest in lime trees began in Sheffield, where the natural distribution of the two species was shown to mark fragments of the original woodlands of Derbyshire. His recently completed monograph of the genus has a global perspective.

References

[1] Clapham, A.R., Tutin, T. and Moore, D.M., *Flora of the British Isles.* Cambridge University Press, 1990.

[2] Trotman, D. in Pigott, C.D. 'The status, ecology and conservation of *Tilia platyphyllos* in Britain', in Synge, H. (ed), *The Biological Aspects of Rare Plant Conservation.* Wiley; Chichester, 1981. pp.305–317.

[3] Babington, C.C., *Manual of British Botany (9th edition).* Gurney & Jackson, London, 1904.

Sources

Pigott, C.D., *Is small-leaved lime native in Scotland or Ireland?* BSBI News No.93, 10–11, 2003

Preston, C.D., Pearman, D. A. and Dines, T.D., *New Atlas of the British & Irish Flora.* Oxford, 2002.

Pigott, C.D. and Huntley, J.P. *Factors controlling the distribution of Tilia cordata Tilia cordata at the northern limits of its geographic range. 2.* History in north-west England, *New Phytologist 84,* 145–164, 1980.

Pigott, C.D., *Lime-trees and basswoods: a biological monograph of the genus Tilia.* Cambridge University Press, 2011

Fig. 1: Large-leaved lime (Tilia platyphyllos)

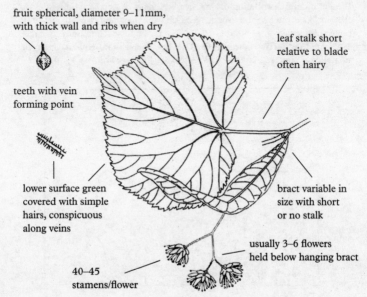

fruit spherical, diameter 9–11mm, with thick wall and ribs when dry

leaf stalk short relative to blade often hairy

teeth with vein forming point

lower surface green covered with simple hairs, conspicuous along veins

bract variable in size with short or no stalk

usually 3–6 flowers held below hanging bract

40–45 stamens/flower

Fig. 2: Small-leaved lime (Tilia cordata)

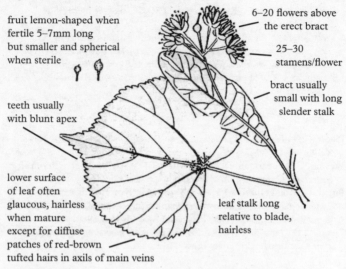

fruit lemon-shaped when
fertile 5–7mm long
but smaller and spherical
when sterile

6–20 flowers above
the erect bract

25–30
stamens/flower

bract usually
small with long
slender stalk

teeth usually
with blunt apex

lower surface
of leaf often
glaucous, hairless
when mature
except for diffuse
patches of red-brown
tufted hairs in axils of main veins

leaf stalk long
relative to blade,
hairless

Fig. 3: Distribution of lime in Northern Britain

Present natural distribution of small-leaved lime at its northern limit in
Britain (black circles) and 'isopoll' lines showing maximum percentages of its
pollen in deposits from 5000 to 3000BC (top isopoll area and outlying circles:
1-4%; middle: 5-10%; bottom: 10-20%). Test sites with infrequent, single, or
no pollen-grains are marked with crosses. See Pigott & Huntley 1980.

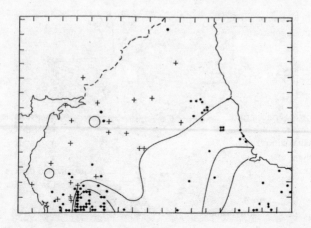

LODGEPOLE PINE
Pinus Contorta

Pinus contorta was one of the pioneers to flourish in the northern hemisphere after the last ice age. The Scottish botanist David Douglas discovered *Pinus contorta var. contorta* in Oregon near the mouth of the Columbia River in 1825 and introduced seeds to Britain in 1831. However, these were lost, or failed to thrive, and the species was reintroduced in 1855, 21 years after his death. John Jeffrey, another Scot, was sent as the Oregon Association's first plant collector to retrace the explorations of Douglas and discovered *Pinus contorta var. latifolia* in 1851. He introduced seeds in 1853, one year prior to his mysterious disappearance on a further expedition.

Where it grows

Pinus contorta is found in three geographical areas in North America, having the largest altitudinal distribution of all pine, tolerating a range of soil pH from 3.6 to 8 and withstanding extreme exposure to wind and wetness.

The name *contorta* is considered by various authors to describe windblown, twisted branches, twisted leaves or twisted buds. Douglas is reported to have named it to describe the appearance of some dead trees in which, he said, 'The branches of these trees curve downwards and inwards, thus reversing the natural upward curve of their extremities while living'.

There are two common varieties in North America, which are also encountered as 'aliens' in many locations throughout the northern hemisphere. *Pinus contorta var. contorta* is also known as shore pine, beach pine, scrub pine, twisted pine or tamarack pine. *Tamarack* is a word that was used by the Algonquin Indians who inhabited areas along the Ottawa River and the northern tributaries of the St Lawrence River. The tree is often low-spreading but can be up to 23m tall. It is usually densely branched and frequently has a forked trunk. It is a native of coastal areas in south-east Alaska, Colorado, Utah and California. When growing in soft terrain, the heavy crown of five-to-ten-year-old trees bends the trunk. Eventually it will resume its vertical growth, giving rise to a permanent butt sweep. Its ability to survive in wet conditions is related to the development of air cavities within the roots.

Pinus contorta var. latifolia is also known as lodgepole pine or Rocky Mountain lodgepole pine and is a native of south-east Alaska, central Yukon, the northern Rocky Mountains and the Black Hills. This wind-firm variety grows at altitudes of up to 3900m. It is a tall tree with a narrow crown, achieving heights of 50m in favourable habitats, and is the most common conifer on the northern Rocky Mountains. The tallest specimen in Britain is about 34m in height.

Two uncommon native varieties are also found in North America. *Pinus contorta var. bolanderi* is a small, broad-crowned tree restricted to the white sand barrens along the Mendocino coast of California. It is an endangered species. *Pinus contorta var. murrayana*, Sierra lodgepole pine, is usually tall, up to 25m, with a narrow crown and is a native of the Cascades and Sierra Nevada.

In Scotland lodgepole pine was tried as a timber tree. Extensive plantations were put in on upland sites during the period 1960 to 1990. In some regions, notably the Highlands, they now account for about 10 per cent of Forestry Commission planting. However, it was observed that the species is prone to wind-throw and to honey fungus and it no longer appears to be much used, even though lodgepole of Alaskan provenance is said to yield timber as good as that of Scots pine.

What to look for

The leaves are mid-green, sheathed in twos (apart from a three-leaved variety of *var. latifolia* found in the Yukon), 3–8cm long and surviving for four to six years. Lodgepole pine bears the longest leaves. The leaves of the coastal form are considered to have more stomata per surface unit than any other conifer, enabling high transpiration rates in wet habitats. Winter foliage tends to become yellow-green, which is related to a reduction in chlorophyll and an increase in carotenoids.

The buds are dark red-brown, resinous, cylindrical, tapered to the apex, and often twisted. The cones appear on trees after the age of about six years. They are asymmetrical, except in the case of the Sierra lodgepole, and are minutely prickled and clustered in whorls of two to four. Those on the shore pine point backwards and open at maturity. Cones on lodgepole pine point outwards and are serotinous, often remaining closed for many years until fire melts the resin, releasing seeds. As such, it is a pioneer species following forest fire.

Lodgepole bark is dark brown to grey, smooth and thin on young trees. This becomes thick and fissured into small oblong plates, which are covered in red-brown scales in maturity. The heartwood is reddish-yellow, while the sapwood is pale yellow. It is finely straight-grained, but may be spiral in shrubby trees. The wood is resinous and knotty.

Uses

The name 'lodgepole pine' is derived from the use of the trunk as the centre pole of the tipi or lodge traditionally built by some Native American peoples. The inner bark of the shore pine was also used as an ingredient in coarse bread, and the sweet orange-flavoured sap of both varieties provided a delicacy, either fresh or in dried form. General uses include fuel, mine timbers, poles and posts, boxwood, flooring, railway sleepers, and pulping for paper and fibreboard. Shore pine provides an excellent shelter-belt in areas exposed to sea winds and on wet land. Choosing the most appropriate provenance of seed is vital in determining the best tree for forest or shelter-belt.

Professor A. M. Martin,

who qualified in Medicine and Bioengineering at St Andrew's
and Strathclyde Universities, has been planting trees in the face of
Atlantic gales in Wester Ross for over 30 years.

Sources

Veitch, J. *A manual of the Coniferae.* London, 1881

Sargent, C.S. *Manual of the trees of North America.* Dover Publications,
Inc., New York, 1922.

Vidakovic, N. *Conifers morphology and variation.* Graficki Zavod Hrvatske,
1991.

Viereck, L.A. and Little, E.L., *Alaskan trees and shrubs.* Forest Service,
United States Department of Agriculture, 1972.

Packham, J.R., Harding, D.J.L., Hilton, G.M. and Stuttard, R.A.,
Functional ecology of woodlands and forests. Chapman and Hall, London,
1996.

MONKEY PUZZLE
Araucaria araucana

Our native trees need to be the backbone of a reforested Scotland, to sustain the biodiversity of our land and continue the visual character of the landscape. There are, however, landscapes that take their character from introduced trees. One area in particular is the landscape around Dunkeld, where old spruces, larches and Wellingtonia tower above the oak and birch and are a wonderful sight.

Many of our introduced trees have been around for hundreds of years – the sycamore (*Acer pseudoplatanus*) was introduced in the 1600s. It is the scourge of some nature conservationists, due to its ability to take over a native woodland, but it nevertheless supports huge amounts of aphids, which are a food supply for summer visiting birds such as warblers. Mature sycamores look just as wonderful as old oak trees. Some of these introduced trees have become part of our cultural heritage: the horse chestnut (*Aesculus hippocastanum*) heralds the seasons, with its white candle flowers in spring and its conkers, an icon of childhood. Another such tree is the monkey puzzle, probably our best-known introduced conifer. Almost every part of the British Isles has its share of these trees, due to the Victorian passion for them.

Distribution
Originally called the Chile pine, this tree is a member of the *Araucariaceae* genus of conifers. There are 18 species in the

southern hemisphere occurring in New Guinea, Australia, New Hebrides, New Caledonia, Norfolk Island and South America.

It is sometimes referred to as a relict conifer, because it dates back over 200 million years. The tree evolved in the Carboniferous period and was one of the earliest seed-producing trees. In the Cretaceous period they were common as giant trees that towered above the forest canopy, along with the podocarps, such as the tree ferns.

The leaves evolved to be small and spiny, to protect against grazing dinosaurs such as iguanadon or triceratops. Around 190 million years ago the trees were one of the dominant species of the southern hemisphere, with a range that stretched from Brazil to Antarctica.

Today, however, Araucaria are found in a very restricted range: two small areas in the Araucaria region of central Chile, and an area of the Andes on the border of Argentina and Chile, situated on the mountains and volcanic slopes.

Some years ago, I made a visit to the Auracaria forests as part of a trip to southern Chile and Argentina. Chile is an extremely long, narrow country, stretching 4350km from the border with Peru (where there are virtual deserts) to Tierra del Fuego (not unlike northern Scotland), which is just 1000km from the Antarctic Circle.

I visited the Huerquehue National Park. The lower slopes of the hills are clothed in southern beech (*Nothofagus pumilio*) along with bamboo and fuchsia. I remember gorging myself on blackberries, an introduction to the park. Between 1000m and 2000m the *Araucaria* grow, and as you walk through the woodlands, you gradually start to see on the skyline the distinctive umbrella canopy. It's a wonderful sight, on reaching 1000m, when the forest changes from the deciduous *Nothofagus* to the coniferous *Araucaria*. The forest feels very ancient, made up only of stands of monkey puzzle, from young ones with their pyramidal shape to ancient ones. Some of the old trees in the forest were between 1000 and 2000 years old and were 50m in height. The BBC used forests such as Huerquehue as backdrops for the series 'Walking with dinosaurs'. There are not many places on Earth that look like a Jurassic landscape, as most of the planet is covered with grass, which was not around at the time of *Tyrannosaurus rex*.

Uses

Ironically, the Araucaria forests do not support monkeys, but do provide a habitat for a number of rare and endangered birds, such as the Chilean pigeon and the slender billed parakeet. The trees also provide food for the indigenous people, the Pehuenche (*pehuen* means 'monkey puzzle', *che* means 'people'). For part of each year, during late summer and early autumn, the Pehuenche live mainly as seed gatherers. The men scale the trees with the aid of ropes and use thin poles to knock down the seeds. The seeds are locally known as *piñones* and form an important part of the winter diet. The Pehuenche also sell part of their harvest, and on my visit I was surprised to see a supermarket selling them, alongside peppers, for about 50p per kilo. They taste like chestnuts and turn pink on boiling. The monkey puzzle is sacred to the Pehuenche and they regard the tree as part of their extended family – *lobpehuen*.

How it was introduced

It was probably seed gathered by the Pehuenche people that led to the tree being introduced to our islands by Archibald Menzies, one of the most celebrated plant hunters of the age. He was the naturalist-surgeon on board Captain George Vancouver's ship, Discovery, in 1795. At a dinner for the Governor of Chile, the guests were offered the Araucaria seed for dessert. Menzies pocketed some, and sowed these nuts on board the ship. Five plants survived the voyage back. Sailing north, Menzies also discovered the Douglas fir (*Pseudotsuga menziesii*), named after that other famous Scottish plant hunter, David Douglas, who discovered the Sitka spruce. One of the original Araucaria survived at Kew Gardens until 1892.

The original trees brought back must have been much prized for their uniqueness. The Cornishman William Lobb was said to have collected up to 3000 seeds in the mid-19th century, which were then grown by Veitch & Sons of Chelsea, London.

It was about this time too that the tree got the name that has stuck to it. Many questions were raised as to how the monkeys of the Chilean jungle were able to get at the edible nuts. 'To climb that tree would puzzle a monkey', people said. From then on it was called the monkey puzzler, later shortened to monkey puzzle.

Conservation

Like many forests, *Auracaria* forests are being destroyed. In 1976 the tree was recognised by the Chilean government as a national monument and given official protection. Widespread illegal felling continued, however, and large areas of the forest were mysteriously set on fire, destroying many ancient habitats. Evolving on volcanic soil led the tree to develop a honeycomb-patterned bark, which can grow up to 18cm thick and may account for 25 per cent of the tree's volume. This enabled the tree to survive the fires and the intense heat of volcanic eruptions, but now they have to face the loggers. The burnt trunks still have timber that can be used for building purposes. In 1987 the government gave way to the pressure from the powerful timber industry and revoked the tree's protected status.

Monkey puzzles are just one of a number of threatened conifers throughout the world. A Conifer Conservation Programme (CCP) has been set up and is based at the Royal Botanic Garden, Edinburgh (RBGE). The aim is to collect seed of threatened species and grow them on safe sites – parks and gardens around Britain and Ireland. These have to potential to play a major role in reintroduction programmes in order to reinforce genetically depleted populations in the wild. A CCP trip was made to Chile in 1997 to collect seed, and 2000 seeds were brought back from more than 60 trees scattered over Chile's monkey puzzle forests. At RBGE they were sown immediately on the top of compost in small pots. After 28 days, 90 per cent of the seeds had germinated. The programme has distributed the plants that have germinated from this batch and several others. In Scotland these plants have been sent to Ardkinglas Estate, Ardross Castle, Benmore Botanic Garden, Cawdor Castle, Kilmun Arboretum, Pitlochry Plant Hunters Garden, Torosay Castle, and Weem

Forest Walk. The tallest saplings RBGE has monitored in these sites are now about 3m tall.

In many respects, the story of the monkey puzzle has come full circle. Just like Archibald Menzies, Scottish plant hunters are again collecting seed, introducing the new exotics to parks and gardens, and again prizing them. This time it is for their potential to reforest the Chilean mountains, although our own urban landscape will benefit too.

Kevin O'Kane
is a Chartered Landscape Architect working for Fife Council.

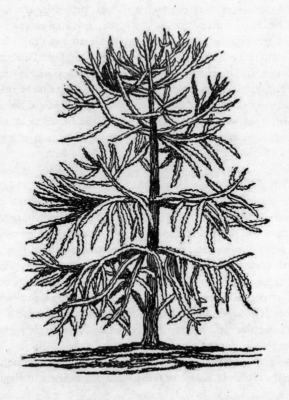

OAK
Quercus / darach

Chief of the seven Celtic Chieftain Trees, prized by the Celts for its beauty, its great size, and its 'pig-fattening acorns', the oak had great importance throughout the history of the Western world until recent times. In old Scots Gaelic and Irish Gaelic the oak is *dair*, and *darach* in modern Scots, with a possible origin in the Sanskrit *drus*, meaning, simply, 'wood'. This Gaelic origin appears in names such as Craigendarroch, the hill above Ballater and Ardarroch on Loch Kishorn. Indeed, the Celtic word *druid* itself comes from the same roots, one possible meaning of which is 'men of oak'.

Where it grows

Oaks are members of the *Fagaceae* family, as are beech and chestnut. Worldwide, the *Quercus* genus is huge, containing more than 450 distinct species of both deciduous and evergreen trees, with over 800 described forms including natural hybrids. The major common link is that they all bear acorns. This genus, found throughout all northern temperate regions of the world, contains species as diverse as the cork oak of Portugal and North America (*Q. suber*), which has traditionally provided the corks for wine bottles, and the red oak (*Q. rubra*) commonly planted here for its autumn colours.

Two species are native to Britain and both are common in Scotland: sessile oak (*Quercus petrea*) and pedunculate or English oak (*Quercus robur*). Both are monoecious, meaning that each tree has both male and female flowers on it. The clearest distinguishing features are the stalks or peduncules on which the pedunculate oak bears its fruit. The acorns of the sessile oak are stalkless, but its leaves are distinctly stalked, unlike the leaves of pedunculate oak, which have none. However, to confuse things, widespread hybridisation does occur.

In Scotland, oak would have held an important place in both lowlands and upland landscapes, wherever soils and aspect favoured it, and some excellent examples remain of productive oak woodland of the highest quality, such as at Cawdor and Darnaway on the Moray coast. An interesting 100ha woodland of possible former coppice also survives at Spinningdale on the Dornoch Firth. With Scotland at the extreme north-western edge of the species' range, the significance of the sessile oaks of the Atlantic oakwoods should also not be ignored. These ancient wildwood remnants form biodiversity-rich temperate rainforests of international significance with their unique variety of bryophytes and other lower plant species. Inspirational examples include woods on the cliff slopes on the west of Arran, hidden in the hinterland of Mull, and clinging to the coast of the far north-west at Loch a Mhuilinn, by Duartbeg, Sutherland.

What to look for

Both native species show fairly slow initial growth (10–20cm a year), so competition from weeds can be a problem. This can be helped by an additional growing period between July and August, known as lammas growth, which is named after Lammas Day (August 1st), the Celtic New Year. Whilst this second growth burst cannot always be relied upon, it can certainly be stimulated either by planting the tree in tree-shelters on appropriate sites, or by creating a similar woodland microclimate to encourage several possible bursts of lammas growth in a single season.

Once fully established, growth speeds up considerably to about 50cm a year on fertile sites. The tree reaches full height at about 100 years, although the stem can continue to increase in girth by about 2.5cm a year for a further 150–200 years. Oak responds well to being cut, either as coppice or pollard.

Unpollarded it may live to around 400 years, but pollarded trees can live for 800 years or more.

Tree shape varies greatly, depending on site and local conditions. Those growing in open woodland have a characteristic domed crown and can reach heights of over 40m. The girth of one specimen, near Wrexham in north Wales, is now some 12.9m around and is known at the Pontfadog Oak, or Gate of the Dead tree. Not dead itself yet, it would appear to be over 900 years old. A well-known ancient Scottish example is the Birnam, or Macbeth oak, which stands on the banks of the Tay at a mere 5.5m around –next to an even more impressive sycamore!

Oak is deservedly famous for the incredibly wide range of life forms it supports. Species include a wide range of mammals and birds, such as the pipistrelle bat (*Pipistrellus pipistrellus*) and the woodcock (*Scolopax rusticola*) and a whole host of insects and lower plants. Examples of these latter include: the wonderfully named and very beautiful *merveille-du-jour* (*Dichonia aprilina*), a lichen-mimicking moth; and the incredibly edible beefsteak fungus (*Fistulina hepatica*), which has blood-like sap, thick succulent flesh and a sour-ish, pleasant smell, and is a parasitic bracket-fungus commonly found at the base of the trunk. As well as being good to eat, this fungus causes a brown rot, which results in a darker, richer colour of timber. This 'brown oak' can command a higher value for sale to the furniture industry. However, not all fungi form beneficial relationships for the tree or woodland managers; one harmful one is the oak mildew (*Microsphaera alphitoides*), which can cause significant deaths in young seedling trees.

The lichens, fungi and insects which live on oak feed many other creatures, often in a symbiotic relationship highly beneficial to the host tree. Perhaps as a result of this generous biodiversity, the oak is remarkably resilient to infestations and plagues, such as those of the leaf-roller moth (*Tortrix viridana*) and the winter moth (*Operophtera brumata*), which both cause widespread defoliation. Another common infestation is that of oak galls, spherical growths on leaf or twig caused by a wide range of organisms, including midges and wasps. Most galls are harmless to the tree, such as the oak-apple gall, caused by the wasp *Biorhiza pallida*. However, knopper galls formed by the wasp *Andricus quercuscalicis* cause considerable acorn losses in mast years. Both wasps lay their eggs in developing tissues, thus stimulating the formation of galls within which the larva lives and feeds.

Another plant well known for its association with oak is the hemi-parasitic mistletoe (*Viscum album*). The white berries of the mistletoe were much revered by the druids, who, on the rare occasions when the plant chose to grow on oak, saw the berries as containing the semen of the oak god. These associations of fertility are echoed in modern mistletoe rituals. Some of its common names of all-heal, birdlime mistletoe and devil's fuge suggest other uses made of the plant.

Where (and which species) to plant

Surprisingly, there appears to be little regional difference in the rates of oak growth of either species. Throughout Britain both species occur on all major soil types. This often results in no distinction being made silviculturally between the two species: an unfortunate fact as sessile does tend to do better on the lighter soils of the north and west, and pedunculate on the heavier clay soils of the south and east. This tendency also suggests areas of native origin, but as oak has been planted in the most remote of locations, the species cannot be comfortably separated geographically.

Whichever you choose to plant, the pedunculate oak is more tolerant of waterlogged conditions, whilst both species appear to dislike strongly calcareous soils. If quality timber is a desired goal, light, freely drained soils should be avoided for both species, as these conditions appear to be associated with 'shake', a condition that can render the wood useless as timber. Site permitting, sessile is increasingly the preferred species, as it tends to give a good, straight trunk that persists high into the crown, with minimal branching. Oak foliage is highly susceptible to late spring frosts and is therefore better suited to sheltered locations, avoiding obvious frost hollows. A suitable companion plant is hazel.

Cultivation

Both species seed in late autumn, producing fruit on trees over 40 years old. Mast years in Scotland, particularly for sessile oak, are erratic and weather dependent. They can be anything from two to five years apart. A mature oak produces up to 50,000 acorns in a good year. Viability is generally high at about 60-80 per cent, though in the wild the seed survival rate can be as low as 0.5 per cent due to predation. Browsing in early years accounts for further seedling loss, as does intolerance to low light levels under its own canopy. Birds such as the jay (*Garrulus glandarius*) therefore play an important role in distributing the seed to canopy gaps and woodland edges where the most favourable conditions exist. Acorns are best planted immediately, covered by a thin layer of leaf litter to preserve moisture. If stored over winter, acorns should be left to dry in a dry place until 'sweating' has stopped, and thereafter lightly sprinkled with water once a month to prevent wrinkling. Storage for more than a year leads to a marked decrease in viability.

Uses

The timber of the two species is virtually indistinguishable and both are marketed as 'English oak'. The heartwood is lignin-rich, therefore deep brown in colour and extremely hard, strong, and naturally durable (and see above, beefsteak fungus, in 'What to look for'). Traditionally, oak is hewn with hand tools, which split the wood cells apart along the medullary rays, leaving no weak points for rain or fungi to enter. This is of particular importance for use in building, whether for ships, houses, or cathedrals. Similarly, cleft oak provides durable material for fencing, roof shingles, ladder rungs and barrel staves. In whisky barrel production, the oak staves undergo an initial firing treatment, which encourages the slow release of various compounds into the whisky, particularly from the lignin. These impart colour and smoother flavour to the drink, whilst the charcoal residues absorb the harsher compounds as the whisky matures.

Sawn oak also has a great variety of uses, particularly in heavy-duty construction work. Sliced or sawn on the true quarter it is often used as a decorative veneer. The 'silver-grain' thus produced is an attractive feature of worked wood when it is used for panelling or cabinet-making.

Oak coppice makes excellent charcoal and the young bark is also rich in tannin, essential in the production of leather. In the eighteenth century, tanbark was an important harvest throughout the Highlands and provided an important link between the farm and the forest, which is all but nonexistent anywhere in Britain today. Cut every 20 to 30 years, coppice also provided wood for products such as fencing, pit-props and thatching spars. There are still some substantial areas of coppice and former coppice woodland remaining in parts of England, and also some notable remnants surviving in Scotland, for example, on Loch Lomond and Loch Ness sides. Very few of the English woods are worked on a regular basis, with the possible exception of the Kent and Sussex coppices, although sweet chestnut is perhaps dominant here. There is, however, growing interest in reviving the tradition and some highly successful local coppice projects exist, especially south of the Border. A good starting point for information might be the Coppice Association North West (of England).

Lore

In cosmologies from the ancient Greeks to the Norsemen, the most powerful gods were symbolised by the oak tree. For the Celtic druids he was Esus, whom they worshipped in sacred oak groves, such as the one which is said to have existed on Isle Maree, where the remains of a wishing tree now lie. Oak was used for ritual fires, such as those for the ceremonies of Beltane, and summer solstice. The oak for the winter solstice fire seems to have become the yule log that was still a distinct feature of Christmas within living memory. In earlier times, and seemingly over a very long period, oak logs were burnt by Highlanders on sacred need-fires in summer.

Steve Robertson
is a former Director of Reforesting Scotland. He is now employed as Forest Trust Manager, North Highland Forest Trust.

Sources

Mitchell, A., *A Field Guide to the Trees of Britain and Northern Europe*. London, Collins, 1988.
Hageneder, F., *The Meaning of Trees*, San Francisco, Chronicle Books, 2005.

Featherstone, A.W., Trees for Life, Species Profiles, Oak:
   http://www.treesforlife.org.uk/forest/species/oak.html
http://www.ancient-tree-hunt.org.uk/discoveries/newdiscoveries/2008/
   queenelizabethoak.htm
http://www.straighttalkpsychics.com/topics/trees/oak.htm
Phillips, R., *Mushrooms*, London, Macmillan, 2006.
http://www.forestresearch.gov.uk/fr/infd-7b3d8v
http://www.globalherbalsupplies.com/herb_information/mistletoe.htm
Edlin, H.L., *Broadleaves*, Forestry Commission Booklet No 20, London,
   HMSO, 1985.
Smout, T.C, MacDonald A.R, Watson, F., *A History of the Native Woodlands
   of Scotland 1500–1920.* Edinburgh, EUP, 2005.
www.canw.woodlandrecollections.org

ROWAN
Sorbus aucuparia / Luis, or Chaoruin

Few other trees capture the spirit of Scottish landscape in the same way as the rowan. It thrives in harsh environments, often seeming to grow out of bare rock, is of value to wildlife, and is steeped in folklore.

Where it grows

The rowan tree is native throughout Scotland, particularly to the north-western and north-east Highlands. It is most abundant on light, acidic soils and is not long-lived in waterlogged conditions or on heavy clay, or on limestone soils. Rowans are often found in inaccessible places, such as rocky outcrops or steep cleuchs, which provide some protection from browsing herbivores and the many small animals that find the shoots particularly palatable. The much-cited ability of rowan to maintain an erect tree form at higher altitudes than any other tree in the British Isles may be partly explained by rapid early growth in response to the short growing season, resistance to winter desiccation, and tolerance of poor soils and exposure. The rowan is associated with the Caledonian pinewoods, although it occasionally occurs in pure stands. It is also a frequent component of ash-rowan and oak-birch woodland communities.

The generic name *Sorbus* originates from the Latin for the sorb apple, and the specific, *aucuparium*, means bird-catching. This refers to an ancient belief that the berries intoxicated birds and made them easier to trap. The vernacular name, rowan, is believed to derive from the Gaelic *ruadh-an*, 'red one', and the Norse *ru*, meaning rune. Other names include *caorthain*, and *fid na ndruard*, 'the tree of the wizard'.

Of the other species of *Sorbus* that occur within the British Isles, only *S. rupicola, S. arranensis,* and *S.pseudofennica* are native to Scotland, the latter two being endemic to Arran, and probably of hybrid origin.

What to look for

The rowan is usually a small, slender tree which reaches a maximum height of 15–20m. Because of its tendency to produce basal shoots, particularly in response to browsing or coppicing, multi-stemmed forms often occur. Root suckering is sometimes reported, resulting in localised thickets of rowan. Flowering occurs from May to June, when the clusters of creamy-white, foetid-smelling flowers are pollinated by flies and other small insects. The characteristic red berries ripen from late August to September, but are quickly devoured by many birds, such as thrushes, ring ouzels, and fieldfares, which distribute the seeds. Bird-dispersal of the seeds is particularly important for the continuance of populations at high altitudes, where viable seed is not always produced. The berries are less than cm in diameter, with tough, shiny skins and mealy flesh. They each contain two seeds.

Where to plant

The rowan performs best on light, acidic soils, so avoid lime-stone, heavy clay, or waterlogged conditions. Because of its ability to form mychorrhizal associations, and its generally tough, fibrous roots, poor soils or even rock outcrops are also suitable for planting. The tree is extremely hardy, and able to tolerate cold, exposure to wind, and even a degree of urban pollution. It is particularly adapted to high altitudes. Along with birch, it is a pioneer species, able to take advantage of vegetation gaps following clear-felling or other catastrophes. Unlike birch (its chief competitor on upland sites), rowan will tolerate some shade, although flowering under such conditions may be sparse. Rowans generally transplant easily, and the roots are fairly resistant to desiccation. However, because of the palatability of the bark and the stems to a host of large and small herbivores, including deer, cattle, sheep, rabbits and hares, it is generally advisable to protect seedlings either with tree guards or by fencing.

How to grow

Seed can be collected as soon as it ripens in late August or early September, before many of the birds that feed on the berries have had chance to strip the trees. The seeds are doubly dormant, meaning that both the seed-coat and the embryo require a period of stratification before germination can take place. The flesh of the berries contains substances which inhibit germination. These may be removed by macerating the berries and washing away the fleshy parts, or by allowing them to rot over winter. It is usually recommended to subject the berries to a warm period for a few weeks before chilling them for three to four months. Seed may be sown outdoors in the autumn, or chilled in the fridge prior to sowing in the spring. High temperatures in the spring may cause the seeds to enter a second dormancy, broken only by more stratification, so it is advisable to sow before mid-April. Not all seeds will germinate in the first year, so it is worth leaving seed trays outside for a second winter, or seedling rows undisturbed until the next year. As the rowan responds well to inoculation with arbuscular mychorrhizas (soil fungi that associate with the roots of a wide range of plant species) it may be beneficial to incorporate some unsterilised soil containing root fragments into the seed trays or rows, to encourage early formation of mychorrhizas.

Uses

Because of the rowan's small stature and often multi-stemmed habit, its timber is of little commercial value, although the compactness of the grain makes it suitable for turning small items, for veneers, or for pulping. In the past it was used for barrel hoops and archers' bows, as well as for small agricultural and domestic implements. Nowadays, the tree is planted as a broad-leaved component of upland shelter-belts, to provide wildlife interest, or simply because it is beautiful. There is increasing commercial interest in the berries, which have culinary and medicinal uses. They can be used to make jelly, fermented to produce wines, and sugar-coated as confectionery. The fruits are particularly rich in Vitamin C and are considered to have astringent and anti-diarrhoeic properties. However, the seeds also contain cyanine-like substances and so should be administered with caution. In eastern Europe and countries of the former Soviet Union, many breeding programmes have been undertaken to improve fruit quality and pharmaceutical properties. No breeding or selection programmes have been carried out in Britain, although variation between provenances suggests there is potential for improvement of this attractive, sacred, but neglected species.

Lore

According to Irish tradition, the first sacred berry was dropped by Tuatha Dae Dannan, the peoples of the goddess Danu, who later became the Celtic deities. Traditionally, rowan was planted beside cairns, stone circles, and homesteads to protect against witches, and was used in many rituals to ward off evil. It was believed to be the sacred tree of Bride, the pagan Great Goddess. The red colour of its berries was seen as having special powers against malevolent forces. The wood, however, was considered to be the most potent part of the tree, and was used to make divining rods, hung above stables and byres, and incorporated into many domestic and dairy items. Cutting down the tree was believed to bring ill fortune; the fate of the Orkneys was thought to be bound up in a single tree, to such an extent that if so much as a single leaf was removed, the island would fall into foreign hands. When road improvements were being carried out in Argyll, the Kissing Tree of Strachur was transplanted to the banks of Loch Fyne, as the civil engineers were anxious about public opinion if they felled it. However, even moving rowans is considered ill-advised, and growing it from seed *in situ* used to be considered a more prudent option.

Catherine Findlay

has a PhD in landscape design from Edinburgh College of Art.
After some years of working with trees she has now retrained as an
occupational therapist.

Sources

Raspé, O., Findlay, C. and Jacquemart, A.-L., *Sorbus aucuparia, Journal of
Ecology 88*: 910–930. 2000.

Findlay C.M., *The role of arbuscular mycorrhizal fungi in the early growth
of rowan (Sorbus aucuparia L.)* Unpublished PhD Thesis, School
of Landscape Architecture, Edinburgh College of Art/Heriot-Watt
University, 1999.

Howkins, C., *Rowan, Tree of Protection*. Addlestone, Surrey, 1996.

Darwin, T., *Sacred Trees in Scottish Folklore*, in *Reforesting Scotland* issue 10,
1994.

Barclay, A.M. and Crawford, R.M.M., *Winter desiccation stress and resting
bud viability in relation to high altitude survival in Sorbus aucuparia L.*,
1982, in *Flora* 172, pp 21-31.

Gordon, A.G. and Aldhous, J.R., *Seed Manual for Forest Trees*, HMSO,
London, 1992.

SCOTS PINE
Pinus sylvestris / Guibhas

The atmosphere inside our native pinewoods is unique. Walk on the fragrant, springy floor of pine needles, between the heather and blaeberry-encrusted hummocks, see the sun reflected in the orange boughs, and you are in a different world. You can hear the breeze hissing through the blue-green canopy and the sounds of birds and squirrels foraging on the flaky, lichen-covered trunks, and then you may glimpse, through the loosely spaced trees, a hint of the hills beyond. There the old 'granny pines' stand as quiet sentinels of a Caledonian Forest, once widespread, now returning as we extend it with our new-found concern for our natural heritage.

The tree's Gaelic name, *guibhas*, crops up in several place names, both in its native form, such as Allt na Ghuibhas in Wester Ross and Glac a Ghuibas by Ardgower, and as Anglicised derivations such as Dalguise and Kingussie.

Where it grows

Within the Scottish range of *Pinus sylvestris*, 'pine of the woods', there is considerable variation. Some sources suggest that there are grounds for a subspecies, *Pinus sylvetica scotica* and there are now seven distinct groupings of native pinewoods recognised, based on biochemical differences.

Scots pine is the most widely distributed conifer in the world, with a natural range extending from inside the Arctic Circle in Scandinavia to the Mediterranean, and from Scotland to Eastern

Siberia. In Scotland, its natural range is now largely confined to the Highlands, where it grows either in pure stands or in mixed stands with downy and silver birch. Woods listed in the Caledonian Pinewoods Inventory cover 18,000 hectares, comprising 84 separate woodlands of varying sizes. The area is made up of scattered remnants in Rothiemurchus, Abernethy, Glen Affric, the Black Wood of Rannoch and around Loch Maree. All these together constitute about 1 per cent of the estimated former area of 1,500,000 hectares of the Caledonian Forest.

What to look for

Though trees on the European mainland grow to 36m tall, Scots pines in the Highlands generally grow to a height of about 20m, with exceptionally tall trees reaching about 27m. The maximum girth at shoulder height can be up to 2.5m. Scots pines will live for 250 to 300 years, though recently a 520-year-old individual was found in a western pinewood remnant. The tree retains a characteristic conical conifer shape for the first 60 to 80 years, after which it develops its familiar trunk and canopy shape. Mature trees exhibit a number of distinctive growth forms, from the tall, straight trunk with few branches below the main canopy to the spreading trees with multiple trunks.

The bark of the Scots pine is built up of many layers, with thick, brown, deeply fissured layers at the bottom of the trunk and thinner, orange-brown, paper-thin layers towards the top of the tree. The needles are grouped in pairs, and seed-bearing cones develop at the ends of branches. The tree bears both male and female flowers, with the female taking two years from pollination to develop into a mature cone. The Scots pine is described as a keystone species for Caledonian pinewoods, meaning that many other species in the ecosystem depend on its presence to survive. The endemic Scottish crossbill derives food from the pine seed, as does the red squirrel. Tree creepers and crested tits hunt the many invertebrates that make homes among the fissures of the bark.

Many mosses and lichens also find a home there. Larger birds, like the black grouse and the reintroduced capercaillie, eat the shoots and buds of the pine. Wood ants, among others, have a symbiotic relationship with the tree. The ants strip the leaf-eating caterpillars of various insects from it, and the tree provides the building materials and the shelter for the ants' large nests. Like most trees, Scots pine has mychorrizal associations at the root-tips with, in Scotland, over 200 species of fungi. These include *Cantherellus lutescens,* a species of chanterelle which only occurs in pinewoods, and a rare hedgehog fungus, *Sarcodon glaucopus.* These symbiotic associations allow the pine access to certain nutrients and minerals, and they enable the fungi to reap the products of the tree's photosynthesis.

A number of rare and special plants also find a home in the pinewoods, twin flower and creeping lady's tresses among them. Although the current numbers of red deer in the Highlands are a hindrance to the natural regeneration of the Scots pine, they do belong in the forest, where the trees provide them with both food and winter shelter.

Cultivation

Under ideal conditions, Scots pine will start to bear seed after 20 years. Mature, tan-coloured cones can be picked from the trees in spring before they open. Cones should not be collected from the forest floor, even if they are closed, as these have already shed most of their seed. Place the seeds on a tray in a warm place such as an airing cupboard. When the cones have opened, shake the tray to dislodge the tiny, winged seeds. The seeds require a high level of light to germinate, so are best sown in a seedbed of well-drained, mineral-rich soil in early summer. Seedlings are ready to be planted out after two to three years, either bare-rooted or with a soil plug.

Where to plant

The best situations are well-drained, mineral-rich soil on hillsides and morainic mounds of ground-up rock left by retreating glaciers. Because of the deer-browsing problem, fencing Scots pine in its early years is essential to establishment. Do not try to plant under existing Scots pine canopy, as this is not a natural regeneration site, the tree requiring more light than is available there.

Uses

Several features of Scots pine wood have made it an ideal construction material. The wood grows relatively quickly, often with tall, straight trunks, and its high resin content means that it is slow to decay. In the past it was much used for the rough timbers of house building, as well as for pit props and telegraph poles. It was formerly used for masts, spars and planking of ships (witness Beinn na Sparra in Glen Affric). The Blitz in London exposed Victorian sewer pipes made out of hollowed-out pine trunks. The resin from the sap was used to make pitch, to seal beer casks and the hulls of boats. Real turpentine is also derived from distilling the sap. Both these processes are still carried out in Scandinavia. The soft wood is also pulped for paper production.

Medicinally, extracts and decoctions of the resin and needles of the pine have been used, particularly as an inhalant to treat respiratory problems, as an expectorant, and also as an antiseptic or disinfectant. Bach Flower Remedies recommend pine to treat despondency, despair and self-condemnation.

Lore

Ancient Greek and Roman mythology relate pines to fertility, though not specifically the Scots pine. Druids are said to have lit fires under the Scots pine at the winter solstice, to celebrate the passing of the seasons and to draw back the sun. Glades of Scots pine were also decorated with lights and shining objects, the star-covered tree being a representation of divine light.

Although Scots pine is the clan badge of Clan Appin, older Scots lore about pines is minimal, the one persistent theme being their use as markers in the landscape. In the Highlands, planted pines are frequently found marking burial places of warriors, heroes and chieftains. In areas further south, where the sight of a Scots pine would have been more unusual, it can be seen to mark ancient cairns, trackways and crossroads. In England they were used not only to mark drove roads but the borders of fields where passing drovers and their herds could spend the night. There is also a suggestion, perhaps fanciful, that they were planted in England by farmers with Jacobite sympathies.

Paul Kendal

formerly worked for Trees for Life. He is now a Field Teacher at Abernethy and Insh Marshes National Nature Reserves and does outreach in Badenoch, Strathspey and Moray.

Sources

Featherstone A.W., Trees for Life, Species Profiles, *Scots pine*: www.trees-forlife.org.uk/tfl.scpine.html

Fife, H., *Warriors & Guardians*. Argyll, 1994.

Frazer, J., *The Golden Bough* (abridged). Wordsworth Editions, 1993.

Mabey, R., *Flora Britannica*, Sinclair-Stevenson, 1996.

Memory Paterson, J., *Tree wisdom*. Thorsons, 1996.

Steven, H.M. and Carlisle A., *The native pinewoods of Scotland*. Oliver & Boyd, Edinburgh, 1959.

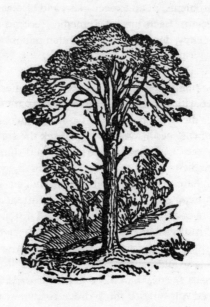

SITKA SPRUCE
Picea sitchensis

Individual reactions to Sitka spruce (*Picea sitchensis*) vary greatly. In British Columbia it has become an icon for the conservation movement. It was the discovery of the Carmanah Giant, a magnificent Sitka spruce over 90m tall, that ultimately led to the prrotection of the last remaining unlogged watershed on the west coast of Vancouver Island. By contrast, in Britain, where huge areas of the uplands have been covered in blanket afforestation with Sitka spruce monocultures, environmentalists concerned with the conservation of nature or landscapes are inclined to loathe it. Hence the surprise of visitors to my office at the time when I had a 'Save the Carmanah Valley' poster on my wall, that the beautiful, moss-covered and evocative trees it depicted were Sitka!

Love it or hate it, you can hardly ignore it, as Sitka spruce represents more than half the trees planted in upland Britain and must now compete with the birch for the most abundant tree in Scotland. Some of the new planting has been with genetically improved 'Super Sitka' propagated from vegetative cuttings, providing environmentalists with extra cause for contempt. Sitka is so at home in the British uplands that it can regenerate within semi-natural vegetation. This has been observed since the 1950s but as more and more young crops reach sexual maturity, we may see an explosion of self-seeded trees invading ecologically sensitive areas.

Where it grows

The natural distribution of Sitka spruce is the 'fog-belt' of western North America, a narrow strip of Pacific coast extending 3000km from northern California to Alaska. In the south of its range it is generally confined to areas below 500m and is often limited to within a few kilometres of the sea. But at the northern end of its range it can be found as a dwarf 'bonsai' tree as high as 1500m. One of the slowest growth rates for Sitka ever recorded was a specimen at the tree limit near the Arctic Circle, which had 100 annual growth rings but was only 28cm tall!

The origin of trees grown in Britain is mostly seed from Haida Gwai (Queen Charlotte Islands) and neighbouring areas of the British Columbia mainland where the wet and cool climate is most similar to that of upland Britain. In its natural home it is generally found in association with Western hemlock (*Tsuga heterophylla*), Lawson's cypress, (*Chamaecyparis lawsoniana*) and Western red cedar (*Thuja plicata*). All of these conifer species also thrive in Scotland, the former in particular regenerating freely on the west coast wherever it has been introduced. Unfortunately Britain has no indigenous species as well adapted to the prevailing cool, wet and windy climate as these introduced American species.

What to look for

The spruces are single-needled conifers most easily identified by the short pegs extending from elongated ridges on the twigs. These persist for a number of years after the needles have fallen. The foliage of Sitka spruce has sharper pointed tips and a more bluish-green colour than the 'Christmas tree' or Norway spruce (*Picea abies*), a European species and the only other spruce likely to be found growing outside an arboretum of garden. The female cones of the Sitka are also shorter than those of Norway spruce, typically only 5–10cm long; the scales have a wavy edge, and the whole cone feels soft when squeezed.

Cultivation

In its natural habitat in North America, Sitka spruce has fairly specific site requirements, preferring water-receiving, 'flushed' sites and deep, fertile soils. However, in the British Isles, although these would still be optimum conditions, the reason for its popularity with commercial foresters is its potential to produce a high-yielding crop under a very wide range of conditions, including waterlogged sites, ironpans, and deep, acidic peats, provided that a sufficient depth of aerated soil is available or can be produced by ground preparation. It is also very tolerant of high levels of exposure and of salt spray.

The silviculture of Sitka in Britain is well known and the Forestry Commission has produced a number of handbooks on the subject, which are readily available. Therefore I offer only a brief summary of current practice. Sitka spruce is invariably grown from nursery-raised transplants or cuttings planted out in late winter or spring. In the past new sites will have been prepared by deep ploughing and drainage, but when restocking clear-felled areas the common practice is to rely on scarification or mounding. The stocking density is usually at 2m spacing, or 2500 plants per hectare.

Herbicide spraying to prevent heather-induced growth check and extensive applications of fertiliser were universal in the past, but there is now often a conscious effort to reduce chemical use under the UK Woodland Assurance Standard, and other methods, including traditional silvicultural practices such as using a nurse crop of pines, may become more commonplace in the future. Except in areas with a high risk of wind-throw, it is recommended that stands are thinned to enhance quality and diameter growth. In the past this regime has not always been adhered to but there is a strong drive to increase thinning programmes to improve quality.

Although it is expected that most Sitka stands, on reaching the expected rotation length of 45 to 60 years, will be clear-felled and replanted, natural regeneration, managed on a 'continuous cover forestry system', is now considered as an alternative. Sitka spruce trees first develop cones at about 25 years of age and after that can produce an abundant seed crop every few years. Regeneration is best under semi-shaded conditions, where there is a mix of organic and mineral soil, although seedling establishment on litter-covered peat has been known. When established seedlings are released by thinning of canopy trees, the resulting advanced growth can form dense thickets where intense competition tends to result in high mortality.

Traditional and modern uses

The First Peoples of the Pacific Northwest made very little use of Sitka spruce timber, preferring the more durable and easily worked wood of the Western red cedar, from which totem and mortuary poles, canoes and longhouses were constructed. Sitka spruce was more highly valued for its roots, which were split lengthwise into four or eight strands for making twined basketry and finely woven waterproof hats. All four sides of their ingenious bentwood chests were made from a single cedar plank, heated to enable the corners to be bent at right angles, and then stitched together, and to the base of the box, with Sitka root strands. The resin of Sitka spruce bark was preferred to the pitch of pines as an all-purpose adhesive, to caulk holes in cedar boats, cure carbuncles, or simply as chewing gum. In Britain the Heather Ale Company has introduced Alba, an ale based on a traditional Highland recipe, which includes the sprigs of spruce and Scots pine.

Although British-grown Sitka is widely regarded as a general-purpose timber, in America trees from old-growth forests have been favoured for a number of specialised uses. Because of its lightness, Sitka was once the preferred wood for aeroplane construction. In the First World War, 10,000 troops (the 'Spruce Division') were dispatched to the west coast of the USA and Canada to supply lumber for this purpose. Today, well-grown trees are highly sought-after by instrument makers for the tops of the best quality violins and double basses. In Britain most Sitka is used for paper pulp, board (for example, chipboard or OSB/oriented-strand board) or construction timber, and increasingly as a fuel wood. On sites less prone to wind-throw, thinning and branch pruning could probably improve the variety of purposes to which it could be applied, but even without pruning it can yield construction timber with stress grades better than we might have assumed in the past.

Most people who object to Sitka spruce plantations do so on aesthetic grounds. However, it is worth pointing out that most of the forested areas are still relatively young. At the 1987 Edinburgh Sitka Spruce Symposium, Professor Roche put it this way: 'It may not be too fanciful to believe that Sitka spruce will prove to be as acceptable to generations of future Britons as the introduced but now homely, and for all practical and aesthetic purposes, indigenous, sycamore. [With] a continued broadening of management objectives, a greater variety of silvicultural systems, and the use of natural regeneration... we can in time create Sitka spruce forests of greater diversity... and with enhanced aesthetic and conservation values... We may not, and perhaps cannot, recreate the splendid spruce forests that David Douglas first saw in North America in 1825, but it would not be a bad thing for British foresters continuing to seek public support for their work, to have them in their mind's eye.'

Dr Ian Edwards

is an ecologist who works for Royal Botanic Garden Edinburgh. He is a former director of Reforesting Scotland and editor of *Woodlanders: New Life in Britain's Forests* (2010).

Sources

Grescoe, A., *Giants – colossal trees of Pacific North America*, Roberts Rhinehart, 1997.

Henderson, D.M. and Faulkner, R. (eds.), *Sitka Spruce* in *Proceedings of the Royal Society of Edinburgh 1195, 93*, pp 1–234, 1997.

Rook, D.A. (ed.), *Super Sitka for the '90s, in Forestry Commission Bulletin 103*, 1997.

SYCAMORE
Acer pseudoplatanus

The sycamore is often referred to dismissively as a foreigner and an invasive weed. But we should really stop scolding this much-maligned tree for a moment and consider its good qualities. For sturdiness and wind resistance it is hard to beat. A sycamore on an exposed hillside grows to symmetrical maturity, where other species become deformed by wind. In cities the sycamore's leaves turn the clearest yellow in autumn (it is not understood whether this is because the leaves are swept away, helping them to avoid fungal infection, or whether pollution does this). You can even tap the tree in February for 'maple syrup'.

Sycamores mature into a diversity of types. Some develop rounded crowns with interestingly crinkly end twigs: these usually also have smaller, shapely leaves, unfolding pale lime-green in spring. Others grow into handsome, more conical trees. An outstandingly distinctive example was the ancient Corstorphine Sycamore, which had very pale leaves. This tree was already very large in 1649, when a murder was committed underneath it, but it was finally blown down in the gale of 26th December, 1998; the main trunk had been hollow for many years. Sycamores also exhibit a wide variation in times of bud-burst in spring, a few leafing much later than the rest. There might be a case for selecting strains that combine the more desired features, including reduced seed-bearing or late-leafing strains for mixed woodlands, to encourage ground flora.

Sycamore is often diligently removed from nature conservation areas, partly because it is invasive and partly because it appears to support fewer insects and other species and because it creates deep shade. However, there is remarkably little direct evidence about the wildlife it can support. It does appear to carry a large total biomass of insect life, even if of fewer species than other trees.

Where it grows

Sycamore's natural distribution includes much of central Europe, mainly in hilly and mountainous regions, as far as the Caucasian mountains, with the exception of Scandinavia. It is difficult to know how far it extended into northern Europe: probably the mainland of Europe adjacent to England was free of sycamore. Therefore natural spread into Britain would have been most unlikely. It is not known for sure when it was introduced: certainly by the mid-sixteenth century, and maybe as early as in Roman times. Since there are regional variations and provenances, there must have been time for these to develop, which points to relatively early introduction. There are some huge trees near Dunkeld in Perthshire, and the Hirsel Estate near Coldstream boasts some of the oldest known.

There has been much discussion about the desirability or otherwise of growing or encouraging this non-native tree. The fact is that it is here and cannot be removed, and it does provide rapid-growing broadleaved shelter, good woodlands where there is little else, and excellent timber.

What to look for

Sycamore is the English name; in Scotland this tree is often called plane, but the true plane is a *Platanus*, as is the US sycamore. The name is probably derived from Greek, *sukin*, meaning fig, and *moron*, or mulberry. The large leaves, with their five lobes, can be confused with the Norway maple; but the latter has a thinner texture with finely pointed lobes and teeth. Once seen, there can be no confusion. The seeds of both species are winged: the sycamore wing is smaller with rounded seed, and the maple larger with flattened seed. The bark of the sycamore varies greatly – for example it is clearly very different in East Anglian and Yorkshire samples (Garfitt, 1995, who gave this as best evidence for Roman introduction). However, in my experience, looking at trees in Scotland, there is a wide range of bark structure from fairly smooth – not unlike beech – to very rough and scaly. The latter is usual in older trees, but age alone does not account for the differences.

Cultivation

Sycamore produces abundant seed in most years and regenerates readily. Clear-cut woods of other species frequently regenerate almost pure stands of sycamore. It is said that rabbits do not eat the seedlings much, so they survive where other species do not. One wonders whether there is ever any need to plant! But being a vigorous and wind-resistant tree, there is a case for planting in exposed areas, roadsides and as shelter. The disadvantage is always that seedlings crop up so readily – but in most places they may do that anyway, without human intervention.

There is some evidence that in healthy mixed-age woodland of native species such as oak, ash and elm, sycamore does not spread so readily and the woods maintain themselves. The problem is the degraded state of the local ecology, which allows sycamore to become the weed that it is, in much the same way that willowherb and docks come to cover derelict and disturbed land. I have seen sycamore in southern Chile, where it does not threaten in the way it does here – presumably because the 40 or so species of local trees regenerate vigorously, and sycamore has less opportunity. This suggests that forest policy should concentrate on regenerating ecologically and species-rich forests, and that sycamore could then fit in as a component without being invasive. An interesting paper suggests that ash can alternate with sycamore by natural regeneration (Waters and Savill, 1992).

Sycamore creates a dense canopy and little will grow underneath it. When thinning in order to make clearances for other species, it is a common mistake not to clear enough; the crowns of semi-mature trees rapidly spread out and shade new plantings.

Growth rates vary greatly with conditions, averaging about 6 cubic metres per hectare per annum, but at much higher rates on good soils. Good quality trees, harvestable for timber, can be achieved in 50 to 70 years. On the other hand, 200-year-old trees, or even older, can provide very high quality fine-grained wood (see below). With such a growth rate and optional short rotation, and high value timber, the value increment per hectare must be much greater than Sitka! Because of this, and especially for potentially "rippled" trees, felling of medium-aged trees should only be for thinning, and good specimens left to grow on, adding more value per year than any new crop.

Sycamore is a favourite with grey squirrels, which cause damage. They ring bark the upper branches when the trees are some 40 years old, sometimes killing the crown. Of course, there is every reason to control grey squirrels beside just this one!

Uses

For the cleanest timber with the characteristic white to cream colour, sycamore should be felled from August to early December. After that, from January onwards, the sap starts to rise and there is a danger of the wood staining a nasty blue-grey in streaks. If you do fell in February, you will see the sap rise immediately, not just under the bark in the cambium and phloem (the nutrient-conducting tissue), but all over the stump. The whole timber will be sodden; this is not consistent with the usual description of timber being dead. Also, even if the centre of the tree has rotted, the rest of the timber retains its whiteness while the tree is standing; yet after felling it rapidly deteriorates unless sawn and dried. How then did it maintain its white quality within the living tree? We have also found that years later, after drying, spring-felled timber seems much more susceptible to woodworm attack, as may be expected from its higher sugar content. Research is clearly needed.

Sawmills usually refuse offers of butts in spring (as did Lothian Trees and Timber, which is now closed), unless they are of exceptional quality and too good to waste. The butts must be sawn as soon as possible, and the boards stacked upright or sideways so as not to touch anything over their whole length, for at least some weeks. Even too much sawdust adhering to the wood will cause dark drying marks. The use of stickers, as is common practice for other timbers, would cause blue staining. Long-term air-drying before kilning is advisable to minimise internal stress, which would be apparent on re-sawing and machining.

Sycamore timber is plain but attractive, becoming a golden colour after being exposed to light for some time. It is easy to work in most hand and machine operations, readily cut in any direction, and produces an excellent finish. While it usually planes to a smooth finish, the valuable rippled sycamore tends to split out the ripples, and shallower planing angles are needed to minimise this. The wood has medium strength, defined as the stress it can stand before rupture, either parallel or perpendicular to the grain. It has low stiffness, meaning it will bend readily, and is excellent for steam bending. Sycamore has very high resistance to abrasion. It is not durable and is unsuitable for use in outdoor environments, unless it is treated with preservatives.

While excellent for furniture and internal joinery, sycamore could be used in many more ways than is generally recognised, even structurally in construction. It is commonly used for domestic utensils like rolling pins and cheeseboards, as well as for butchers' blocks. It can also be nailed (it helps to pre-drill when using wire nails, but American-style hardwood nails should be more suitable). With its abundance and quality in Scotland, the timber should be promoted more.

The rippled or figured sycamore is highly valued for veneers and craftwork. The use of sycamore for musical instruments dates back centuries, and it remains the preferred material for the violin and viol families. Translated into German it becomes *Ahorn* (or Berg *Ahorn*) and translated back, 'maple'. Many are the British violin makers who appreciate good maple from Germany, little realising that it may well have come from Scotland! The violin-making tradition (and school) in Mittenwald in the Bavarian Alps was founded on the sycamore in the mountains. Hans Fuchs, a German dealer from Mittenwald, used to visit Scotland regularly. He would buy up any good, rippled sycamores he could find from north of Newcastle, since the ones from more southerly locations were not suitable for violin making. The stability and long-term survival of the timber is substantiated by the long survival of seventeenth- and eighteenth-century violins, whose quality remains the standard against which modern ones are compared. For this purpose the grain must be straight, the tree preferably grown on level ground so as to minimise any internal strains, and it must be free from stained ring faults. Most Scottish rippled sycamore is still exported to Germany, to Italy for veneers, and to Japan.

The rippled pattern seems to occur in groups of trees – find one and you're likely to find others nearby. Whether the effect is environmental or genetic, or a combination of both, is not known.

Ulrich Loening & David Hadley

were directors of Lothian Trees & Timber (closed in 2009). Ulrich Loening is a biologist who researched and taught at Edinburgh University, finally becoming Director of the Centre for Human Ecology there, until he retired in 1985, when he set up Lothian Trees and Timber. His purpose was to raise awareness and use of local Scottish woodlands and their timber. He continues to write and lecture about ecology and forestry.

Sources

British-grown Hardwoods : the Designer's Handbook. TRADA Technology.

Evans, J. *Silviculture of Broadleaved Woodland,* Forestry Commission Bulletin 62, 1984.

Garfitt, J.E. *Natural management of woods – continuous cover forestry.* Research Studies Press, Taunton, 1995.

Farmer, R.H., Maun, K.W. and Coday, A.E. *Handbook of hardwoods,* HMSO, 1970s.

Informationsdienst Holz, Blatt 80 Ahornholzer Verein Deutscher Holzeinfurhauser, Hamburg, 1987.

Mitchell, A. *A field guide to the trees of Britain,* Collins, 1974.

Waters, T.E. and Savill, P.S. *Ash and sycamore regeneration and the phenomenon of their alternation,* Forestry 65 (4), 417-433, 1992.

WHITEBEAM
Sorbus aria and Sorbus rupicola

The whitebeam is native to Scotland: it has been growing as a wild tree here for thousands of years. There are many forms and sub-species across the British Isles, with a bewildering range of local variations. In Devon and Lancashire, for example, several distinct forms of whitebeam are to be found growing quite close to each other, forms which are very closely related yet remaining distinct, generally only cross-fertilising with others of their form, although cross-fertilisation is an element in the evolution of local variations. The endemic Arran whitebeams (*Sorbus arranensis* and *S. pseudofennica*), found only on that Scottish island, seem to reflect the evolution of both the whitebeam and the rowan (*Sorbus aucuparia*). These rare and special whitebeams deserve an article of their own. Here we are dealing only with the common whitebeam (*Sorbus aria*) and its very close cousin, rock whitebeam (*Sorbus rupicola*). It is interesting to note, however, that the whitebeam and all its peculiar local variants are thinly distributed and only locally common, and tend to be found in remote and relatively harsh environments.

Where it grows

The whitebeam is among the very rarest of native Scottish trees. Unlike other scarce trees, it does not grow particularly in the periphery to the north and west; it is more a tree with a naturally thin and scattered spread. Thus you might find a few in Ayrshire, then see none as you move north up the west coast, but come across sudden groups in the islands of north Argyll. Or you might find it in the gorges of East Lothian and Berwickshire, then see hardly any going north, but find a surprisingly large number in the Aberdeenshire glens. It is very rare in the far north, in the central Highlands and in the high interiors of the Borders and Galloway, but it can be said to be native to most regions of Scotland. Planting and resultant self-seeding masks the natural wild spread to some extent, but pollen samples and other data indicate that its current distribution in the wild corresponds to its natural distribution over the last five thousand years or more.

Like rowan, whitebeam is a pioneer and woodland-edge tree. It is fairly light-demanding and is one of those trees which, in Britain as a whole, favour lime-rich lowland areas but also tend to inhabit the bleakest positions within the periphery of their distribution (where *S. rubicola* is particularly well adapted). The hairy undersides of the leaves resist pollution and salt winds and help the tree to avoid desiccation. Naturally occurring whitebeam species are absent from almost the whole of Argyll – even the most fertile or wooded areas – but can be found on the exposed rocky cliffs of the islands of Lismore and Kerrera. Here in its northern domains, the whitebeam shuns the fertile sheltered places and the dense woodlands of oak, hazel and birch, preferring instead to thrive or survive in isolation, where there are no other large plants to compete with. Paradoxically, the whitebeam is found in woodland further east, for instance in the birch/rowan/cherry woods of mid Deeside. It might be that these whitebeams are closer to pure *Sorbus aria*, yet it may also be that many of these specimens are from planted stock.

What to look for

The whitebeam is a fairly small tree, rarely exceeding 12m in height. Its trunk is rarely more than a metre across and, like the rowan, it will usually branch out a couple of metres from the ground, fanning out into a wide, even and rounded canopy. The bark is a pale shiny grey, similar to rowan but even shinier. The single leaves are large, oval and very slightly lobed, and conspicuously white underneath, giving the tree its name. In May/June, it bears bi-sex flowers in domed clusters, like the rowan though somewhat smaller, followed by bright red fruits in late summer. The fruits are a little larger and less numerous than those of the rowan and they are slightly longer than they are broad.

Cultivation

Collect ripe fruits from September into October. If there has not been any significant early frost, place your fruits in a freezer or store them out of doors, in sand to protect them from birds and mice. You can sow them straight into the ground but rotting may be a problem and they will be vulnerable to creatures foraging over the winter months. You may prefer to keep your fruits in the freezer or sand until early spring, or sow them into the ground or trays in mid-winter. A good mixed soil is ideal, with a little sand, a little peat or acid equivalent and some leaf mould. Sow about 2.5cm deep, either broadcast or in lines, with 2.5cm or more between seeds. Thin out and line out the seedlings in the second or third year and lift for planting a year later. For bringing on more mature specimens for later planting, leave them a further year. Ideally, do not plant out until four years old or more. Otherwise, plant them more or less wherever you like – high places, damp places, slightly acidic or slightly alkaline. They are compatible with most of our native trees and they have ornamental and amenity qualities and ecological value. With their short stature and resistance to exposure, they are, together with Swedish whitebeam (*S. intermedia*), useful trees for planting on exposed, particularly coastal, sites.

Uses

Although the hard, tough wood was used alongside hornbeam for making cogs in early machinery, and the berries were once made into jelly for eating with venison, the whitebeam is not widely valued as a source of timber or other products. Among the most likely reasons for this are its rarity and relatively low-grade timber quality. The timber of any tree can be useful, but whitebeam wood is not long-lasting and other more common trees will generally serve better. The branches and coppice regrowth of whitebeam will also be beaten for quality and availability by other trees.

Lore

Quality is one thing, but rarity and local scarcity would seem to be significant factors in determining traditions. In this the whitebeam again parallels the rowan. The rowan is, of course, more widespread, but is also spread thinly and is locally scarce. The rowan has a long history of taboo against its use and the whitebeam may have acquired similar observance because of its rarity and unfamiliarity.

Hugh Fife
is a long-standing member of Reforesting Scotland and one of the main instigators of the Blarbuie Woodland Project in Argyll, which he co-ordinates.

Gordon Gray-Stephens
is Director of Scottish Native Woods and Secretary of AGWA.

WILLOW
Salix sp. / Shelloch

Most people are familiar with willows and would be able to say what they look like, even though their descriptions would probably vary enormously!

Where they grow

Willows are a complex and varied group of trees: worldwide, there are thought to be somewhere between 300 and 500 species. They can be found in every continent except Australasia, although they are most frequent in the temperate areas of the northern hemisphere. Meikle, a leading authority on willow, says, 'Willow hybrids certainly outnumber those of any other genus in the British flora', and reminds us that there isn't just one willow but many.

For most people the weeping willow is the variety that instantly comes to mind. This tree with its long sweeping branches was brought over from central Asia in the 18th century. Since then it has been widely planted as an amenity tree in cities, parkland and gardens. However, in rural areas the crack willow is a more frequently planted tree. With its short, stout trunk and an orange tinge to its crown in winter, crack willow is a distinctive boundary tree on riverbanks and the borders of agricultural land, especially in the lowland soils of southern Scotland.

What to look for

Willows, along with poplars, belong to the *Salicaceae* family. Estimates of the number of willow species in Britain vary, but Meikle and Brendell both list 18 as being native. The flowers are in the form of a catkin, with the male and female flowers being borne on separate trees. They usually have simple, single leaves, which arise from the stem alternately; however, the shape and size of the leaves vary markedly between the species. Willows have very small, wind-pollinated seeds, which require damp, bare earth for successful germination. These conditions, once frequent along riverbanks and cleared land, are now becoming rarer. Willows are light-demanding species and were some of the earliest pioneers to recolonise the land after the last ice age. They grow in a range of forms: as trees and robust shrubs, e.g. crack willow; as shrubs, such as the sallows and osiers, and as dwarf arctic or alpine willows. The boundaries between the species are weak and this results in frequent hybridisation, with more than 30 recognised hybrids in Britain. Of course, this makes identification no easy matter. Because of the large number of species, their variation in form and the wide range of habitats they occupy, the willow genus as a whole supports 450 invertebrates, more than both species of oak. They are highly palatable to insects and animals alike.

Osiers

Osiers are the subgroup of willows most frequently used by basket makers and craft workers. Three varieties are common in Scotland: the common osier, purple osier, and almond-leafed willow. They tend to be shrubs that produce long, slender stems and have distinctive long, narrow leaves. The common osier is relatively widespread throughout most of Scotland except the far north and the extreme western isles. The purple osier is frequent on the west coast and in southern Scotland but declines in number towards the north and east. The distribution of the almond-leafed willow is generally limited to southern and south-west Scotland. In the past, all these osiers would have been widely used for craftwork. Fisherman would have a few shrubs planted at the lochside near their jetties; travellers would often establish them at their campsites; and crofters would use them for sturdy agricultural creels.

Sallows

Another subgroup is the sallows, a series of shrubs with the odd small tree. They are widely distributed throughout Scotland and some are well recognised, including goat willow, grey sallow, and rusty sallow. They can be seen in hedgerows, woodland edge, wasteground and damp marshy areas.

Montaine willows

Finally, in Scotland we still have remnants of what was once an extensive willow scrub zone on mountainsides and above the tree line. This includes some of the dwarf sallows, such as the woolly willow (*S. lananta*), a low creeping shrub which is now only found in restricted areas of the central Highlands. Other species such a *S. lapponum and S. myrtillifolia* are a little more widely distributed. The smallest, *S. herbacaea*, with its creeping stems and bright green, glossy leaves, does not look much like a tree species at all.

Cultivation of a small to medium willow bed

Willows are fairly difficult to propagate from seed, the seed being very lightweight and delicate. However, if you are keen to propagate unusual varieties such as the montaine willows from stock that would not stand having cuttings removed, it can be done. The right moment for picking willow seed is when small white tufts are just starting to emerge from the catkins. Pluck twigs and store them with their heels in a jar of water until the moment that the catkins start to dehisce. This means that the white tufts will expand into a weak jelly with tiny dots of seeds in it. Prepare a tray of compost and, taking one twig at a time, water the catkins with a fine spray, all the time moving the twig to spread the jelly over the compost without attempting to touch it. Repeat for each twig. Make sure the surface of the compost stays moist by covering it with clear plastic. In a few days the seeds will start to germinate. They will still be small at the end of the year but will be ready for pricking out the following spring.

Growing from cuttings is much more straightforward. When starting to grow craft willows it is useful to develop a small test bed. If you monitor its success over a couple of years, you will find out the snags inherent in your site before before you invest a lot of time and money in establishing a larger area of willow. Your test bed can then act as a future supply of cuttings for any larger plantings you do.

Willow cuttings are relatively easy to take, although gaining good establishment is more of a challenge. Cuttings should be at least 23cm long and at least the thickness of a pencil. They should taken from a mature, healthy tree in the dormant season only after the leaves have fallen. The top cut should be made just above a bud and at an angle, and the bottom cut should be made below a bud and be flat. They can then be planted during the winter into a well prepared bed. If the aim is to produce willow for craftwork, then the cuttings must be grown fairly close together; this results in the nice long, unbranched stems needed for basketry. When pushing the cutting into the ground only a small amount of it should be visible above the ground surface: 6-8cm or just three buds. This allows a greater surface area of the cutting to form a rooting system below the ground level. When planting the cuttings, make sure they are pointing in the right direction, which is with the slanted cut uppermost. It has to be said, however, that even if cuttings are mistakenly planted upside down they have been known to shoot!

The willows should be left for at least two years so that the new root systems can establish themselves. The shoots can then be coppiced annually as they will provide 1–3m of growth each year depending upon the vigour of the species. If you are on a weedy site and choose to coppice your willows down to ground level each year, you will have to ensure that you have an effective means of weed control, as some weeds will out-compete the new shoots on the coppice stool and smother it.

Another option is to grow your willows as miniature pollards; in some areas these were known as shanks because they were cut at mid-thigh height. The willow cuttings are left to grow on for at least five years in order to produce small trees or shrubs. The main trunk is then cut at an angle about 80cm above the ground. The new growth produced each year will then be above the height of the weeds and also beyond the reach of rabbits. When planting willows in order to develop coppice stools, the minimum spacings are 20–30cm between the cuttings and 50–60cm between the rows. This is quite a dense spacing and it can be difficult to get in to weed and harvest the willows. When establishing pollards they are grown at distances of 60–70cm between the cuttings and 70–100cm between the rows.

It is important to take account of aspect, shade, rainfall, soil fertility, weed growth and grazing pressure. We will consider each of these in turn.

Aspect

Willows are not shade-tolerant: they require plenty of sunlight, so the bed must be situated on open ground. Too much shade can curtail growth completely or cause the willow to head towards the light and develop a pronounced kink at the base of the rod. If you are planting a mix of different species in the bed then the more vigorous species, such as *Salix viminalis*, should not shade out the slower-growing willows, such as *Salix purpurea*. So if you were planting on a south-facing slope the *S. viminalis* should be at the top of the slope and the *S. purpurea* at the bottom. If planting quite a wide variety of species, it is important to know the vigour of each one in relation to the others, as it is all too easy to shade out one species grown between two more vigorous ones. Even varieties of the same species can have very different growth rates.

Soil

Basketry willows prefer damp but not waterlogged conditions. They cannot generally withstand summer flooding, which can cause serious damage to a crop. They tend to thrive on deep, fertile soils with adequate drainage. The major osier production region in Britain is Somerset. Somerset has ideal conditions for willows, with a low-lying flood plain, a high water table, and with soils consisting of estuarine peat overlain with varying depths of clay and silt. In areas with well-drained, sandy soils or on sloping ground, a lack of soil moisture can become a problem in dry summers. This can usually be overcome by choosing an appropriate mulch, or it may be necessary to water in the summer.

Weed growth

Speaking from personal experience this can be a major ongoing problem, especially if taking an organic approach. Both the young cuttings at the establishment stage and the coppice stools in later years can be very susceptible to weed competition. There are several ways of dealing with this difficulty, including various choices of mulch to put on the ground prior to planting the cuttings:

- Black plastic: sheets of silage plastic can be obtained from agricultural suppliers. These sheets should be trenched in around their edges and weighted down with stones between each cutting. This prevents vigorous weeds from pushing up the plastic over the top of the cuttings. When pushing the cuttings into the plastic don't cut a slit or cross first: you should be able to push the cutting straight through the plastic into the ground. If the ground is hard or a bit stony, use a pinch bar (of small diameter) and hammer. However, there are a number of problems with black plastic. It will not allow any moisture through, so use only on a damp site. Over time the leaf mould from the willows builds up on top of the plastic rather than rotting down and replenishing the soil below them. The black plastic should be removed after three to four years, once the willow cuttings have thoroughly established themselves. However, if the weed growth is of a very vigorous nature then it may still outcompete the new shoots produced by the coppice stools at the start of each season

- Woven plastic sheeting such as teram can be an alternative to black plastic. It inhibits weed growth but allows rainfall and rotted leaf mould to penetrate.

- A bark mulch consisting of a layer of fine chips with a layer of coarse chips on top provides a biodegradable mulch, but it can tend to rob the soil of nutrients to begin with.

- Old wool carpets weighted down with stones can provide a temporary mulch.

- Damp cardboard weighted down with wood shavings.

- If enough space is left between the rows, they can be weeded by hand with a mower and the clippings left as a mulch.

The willow can also be grown as miniature pollards, keeping the new shoots above the height of the weeds.

Grazing pressure

Most willows are highly palatable to herbivores. The main exception is *S. purpurea,* which has such a high level of salicin that it is known as the bitter willow, and rabbits and deer will leave it alone. Grazing pressure can seriously damage a willow bed so any deer or rabbits must be fenced out.

Pests and disease

Willows are hosts to a very wide range of insects and fungal diseases. Sprays are available to deal with some of them but, as many of these maladies are species-specific, planting a mixed bed can mitigate the problem.

Uses

Willows tend to be very vigorous trees that grow rapidly under the right conditions. As a result the timber is usually light and rather soft and its quality can vary according to the form of its growth. The timber of *Salix alba [var caerula]*, whilst being light, is also quite tough and resilient and was therefore prized for making cricket bats. The most well-known uses of willows are probably in basket weaving, hurdle making and for garden structures. Osiers are most frequently used in these crafts. They can produce shoots that are light, long, and flexible. When woven, they create a strong, lasting structure. The bark of willows was at one time peeled for use in the tanning industry, but this is largely achieved through chemical processes today. If oak and Scots pine were not available, crack willow would be used in the production of small, lightweight boats. Today willows are being increasingly used in riverbank and soil stabilisation projects. Live willow hurdles called 'spilings' may be woven *in situ* to form a protective, growing barrier to the edge of a bank. Because of their vigorous growth rates they have become the chosen species for many biomass trials throughout the country. Willow clones can grow to a phenomenal size over a three-to-five-year period, after which they are coppiced to provide fuel for small power stations.

Medicinal uses

The medicinal and healing properties of willows have long been known and are widely used. The active ingredient in willow, found in the bark, is salicin. It has been used for pain relief, rheumatism and as an anti-inflammatory. The Romans recommended the sap from certain willows as a contraceptive, but there is no evidence that it was effective. The catkins were once used as dressings for small wounds.

Lore

There is an enormous body of folklore, traditional rites and magic associated with willows. The phrase 'knock on wood' has evolved directly from 'knock on willow', and was used to invoke the protective powers of the tree. Willows were often associated with the moon and feminine energy. A peeled white wand of willow was supposed to represent the magic wand of Bride. A white rod was also used as a powerful symbol of justice and as such was carried by the Lord of the Isles at major events. Willows have always had an important role to play in the ecology of the countryside, our everyday timber needs and our traditions and local customs and will no doubt continue to do so well into the future.

Jane Wilkinson
is a weaver of traditional baskets, coracles and hurdles and is a member of the Scottish Basketmakers' Circle. She also teaches these skills and works with children as a Forest Schools teacher.

Sources

Hugh Fife, H., *Warriors and Guardians*, Argyll Publishing, 1994.
Darwin, T., *The Scots Herbal, the Plant Lore of Scotland*, Mercat Press, 1996.
Meikle, R.D., *Willows and Poplars of Great Britain and Ireland*, Botanical
    Society of the British Isles, 1984.

YEW
Taxus baccata / Iubhar

There are ten species of the genus *Taxus*; they are widely distributed throughout the northern temperate zone of the Old and New World. Although classified by many authorities with conifers, the yew lacks the typical seed-bearing cone structure of conifers and does not have resin canals in the wood and leaves. Consequently, it is placed into its own separate taxonomic order, *Taxales*.

In Britain, the principal (and only native) species is *Taxus baccata* – the common yew. The name 'yew' is derived from the Welsh *yw*, which is also related to the Gaelic *iubhar*. It can grow up to a height of 20m in sheltered locations, but is more usually found as a relatively small, bushy tree between 4 and 9 metres tall. The girth of ancient yews can be as much as 10 metres.

What to look for

Yew is evergreen, with needles that are dark green and glossy on the upper side and light green and dull on the underside. They are up to 2cm long, ribbed, soft and blunt.

Yew is dioecious (plants bear either male or female flowers), with flowering in late winter/early spring and fruiting from September to November. Male flowers are small and borne beneath the shoot, while the female flowers are small and green and borne on the end of the shoot. The grey-brown seed is surrounded by the characteristic bright red fleshy aril. The young bark is reddish-brown, turning greyish-brown with age and peeling off in thin scales. Its trunk is often short and uneven, with deep fluting in older trees, and the crown usually dense and heavily branched.

Many yews in Scotland display a natural tendency for the branches to weep to the ground and layer, thereby surrounding the mother tree with an ever-perpetuating ring of live, vigorous foliage. This survival mechanism can be seen to good effect on several exceptional old trees, such as the ones at Ormiston Hall and at Whittinghame Estate, both in East Lothian.

So-called 'Irish yews' (*T. baccata 'Fastigiata'*) with their dark foliage, shorter twigs and distinctive upright appearance are known also as 'fastigiate yews'. They were all vegetatively propagated from a single mutated tree discovered in County Fermanagh in about 1770. The Westfelton Yew (*T. baccata 'Dovastoniana'*) was also discovered around this time in Shropshire and is readily recognisable by its distinctive, widely spreading shape. Several golden-foliaged varieties also exist. These clones will not breed true: their offspring revert to the familiar form of the common yew.

Distribution

The natural range of common yew extends across Europe and Asia Minor to Persia. In Britain it occurs across a wide range of site types up to the northernmost stand of natural yew on a rocky hillside near Ardnamurchan. Yew woods thrive best on the steep chalk slopes of southern England, and what is acknowledged as the finest yew forest in Europe is found on the chalk downland of Kingsley Vale in Sussex. Yew is found as a component of National Vegetation Classification types W8 (ash woods); W10 and W11 (oak woods); W12, W14 and W15 (beech woods); W13 (yew woods); and W21 (hawthorn scrub), where it normally occurs as individual specimens or, more unusually, as small groves.

Yew was widely planted in the nineteenth century to provide an evergreen understorey in many policy plantings associated with large houses. Indeed, it is with ancient family seats, houses and castles that most of Scotland's yews are closely associated. Unlike England, it was only in relatively recent times that planting yews in Scottish churchyards became fashionable. Irish yews, however, are now a familiar sight in these locations.

Propagation

Yew seed can be sown immediately after collection, but germination is uneven. It is better sown in early spring or after two winters of stratification. Seedlings grow slowly and so will need three to four years in the nursery before being planted out. Yew can also be propagated from cuttings taken in autumn or winter. Twigs of 10cm length, with leaves on 20–30 per cent of the length, are successful, although care must be taken to protect cuttings from bright sunlight and drying winds.

Uses

The timber of the yew is tight-grained, extremely hard and very resilient, qualities which endear it to woodworkers. The rich, red heartwood and attractive character of the grain has been much prized by wood-turners for centuries for the production of bowls and decorative objects. More recently it has become sought after as a valuable veneer in cabinet making, although the natural form and growth habits of the yew makes straight, clean stems hard to come by.

In days of old, yew had a much more utilitarian use than it does today. The oldest known wooden implement is a spear made of yew that was found at Clacton-on-Sea and is estimated to be around 250,000 years old. More famously, yew has been the traditional material for the construction of longbows. These were cut and fashioned in a specific manner that relied on the clear distinction between the dark, red heartwood and the light-coloured sapwood. The sapwood has excellent qualities under compression and is used on the inner face of the bow next to the string, while the highly elastic heartwood, with its great tensile strength, is confined to the outside. Taken together, this combination creates a remarkable natural spring that has been employed for centuries to deadly effect.

The Latin name *Taxus* comes from the verb *texere*, to weave. The bast (inner bark) was used for braiding and weaving. The toxicity of yew to humans and animals is well known. All parts of the tree are poisonous, with the exception of the red, fleshy aril. Cattle, sheep, horses and other livestock are known to be particularly vulnerable, and great care must be taken to avoid them coming into contact with any part of the yew. Oddly, deer are known occasionally to browse on yew foliage, apparently with no ill effect. Serious cases of human poisoning are extremely rare. In recent years interest has been focused on the medicinal qualities of yew and in particular on the extract known as Taxol, which shows promise in the treatment of cancer. Yew is a tree capable of causing great harm but also great benefit.

Yew responds well to clipping and has played a significant role in garden design, where it is frequently used for topiary. It also makes a tight, springy hedge.

longevity

Yew is an extremely long-lived tree, capable of attaining great age. Indeed, the oldest living organism in Europe is the ancient tree growing in the churchyard of the Perthshire village of Fortingall. Estimates vary widely, but based on its girth of more than 16m before the heartwood decayed and the trunk began to split, it is thought to be in the region of 3000–5000 years old. Legend has it that Pontius Pilate was born in Fortingall while his father was stationed there as a Roman envoy and that he played in the branches of the yew tree as a child. Scotland is home to many other ancient yews, several in excess of 1000 years in age. Determining the age of yew trees is a very inexact science; growth rates are very slow and extremely erratic and inconsistent.

lore

The great longevity of the yew coupled with the evergreen foliage has resulted in it becoming a symbol of immortality and life after death. It is commonly found in churchyards where it is associated with ancient sites of worship. In many cases, such as that at Fortingall, the yew was not planted near the church, but rather, the church was built near a sacred yew. The ancient Druids associated the yew with death, burial and worship, a practice that seems to have been continued by the early Christians. With the yew's remarkable longevity and its capacity to renew itself from decay, it is easy to see why it became identified with immortality and was believed by ancient peoples to be a symbol of everlasting life. This in turn gave rise to the concept of the yew as the Tree of Life.

In Scottish tradition it is claimed that when holding a branch of yew in his left hand, a clan chieftain could openly insult an enemy so that only those around him could hear, whilst his unfortunate adversary was none the wiser of the abuse.

Donald Rodger
is an independent consultant specialising in the care and management of amenity trees and woodland, who has carried out research into Scotland's ancient and heritage trees.

Nick Marshall
is an Environmental Consultant and a former Development Officer at Reforesting Scotland

Sources

Baxter, T., *The Eternal Yew*. Self-published, 1992.

Bevan-Jones, R., *The Ancient Yew*. Windgather Press, 2002.

Browne, D., *Our trees – a guide to growing Northern Ireland's native trees from seed*, CVNI, 1998.

Chetan, A. and Brueton, B., *The sacred yew*. Penguin Arkana, 1994.

Hartzell, H., *The yew tree: a thousand whispers*. Hulagosi, 1991.

Mitchell, A., *A field guide to the trees of Britain and Northern Europe*. Collins, 1974.

Rodwell, J., *British plant communities Vol 1: Woodlands and scrub*. Cambridge, 1998.

Stokes, J. and Rodger, D., *The Heritage Trees of Britain and Northern Ireland*. Constable, 2004.

Note
Every part of the tree except the red flesh of the berry is poisonous.

APPENDICES

Key facts and figures about Scotland's trees

Responsibility for forestry is devolved to the Scottish Parliament. Scotland accounts for more than three-fifths of the UK's coniferous woodland area and around a quarter of the UK's broadleaved woodlands, as can be seen below. (The figures for these graphs are taken from the Forestry Commission UK's forestry statistics 2014, which have just been released at the time of going to press.)

Whilst total forest cover in Scotland is more than three times greater than it was at its lowest point a century ago (approximately 17% in 2007 compared with 5% in 1900, according to Scottish Natural Heritage), we still compare very unfavourably with other countries in Europe and around the world. The authors of the Scottish Forestry Strategy document published for the government in 2006 called for the forested land area to increase to 25% by the second half of this century. Conservationists are calling for deer numbers to be significantly reduced in order to help achieve this.

Area of woodland by ownership and forest type at 31 March 2014

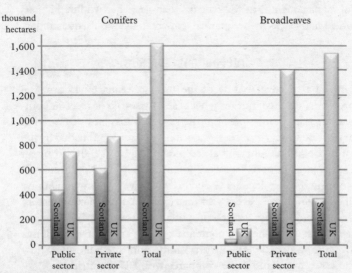

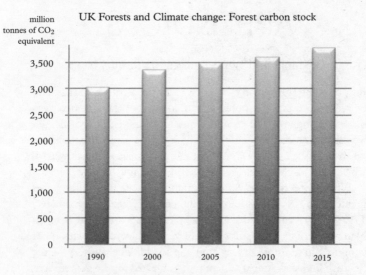

million tonnes of CO_2 equivalent

UK Forests and Climate change: Forest carbon stock

The graph above shows that steady progress is being made in adding to the UK's forest stock. For Scotland to achieve its goal of 25% coverage, between 10,000 and 15,000 hectares of new woodland would need to be planted per year, including 2,000 hectares on the national forest estate, according to SNH. This needs careful management, but the benefits include richer wildlife habitats where native species are planted and greater carbon sequestration.

International forestry

Loss of tree cover is one of the most pressing environmental problems we face, not only because of the role of trees in combating carbon emissions, but the resultant loss and degradation of soil and water resources. According to figures published by the United Nations, our global tree cover has been reduced by an area as large as Peru – 130 million hectares (or 1.3 million km^2) – during the last decade. Globally, we'd have to plant something like 14 billion trees every year for 10 consecutive years to restore this amount of lost forest – or, put another way, each person on the planet would have to plant and care for at least two seedlings a year for a decade. The graphs on the opposite page show how the UK's woodland cover compares with EU countries.

A Handbook of Scotland's Trees

Area of woodland by country in the UK and EU

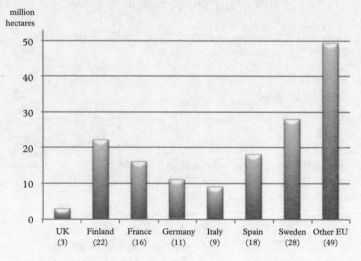

Source: Forestry Commission statistics 2014

Area of woodland by country in the UK and EU per 100 population

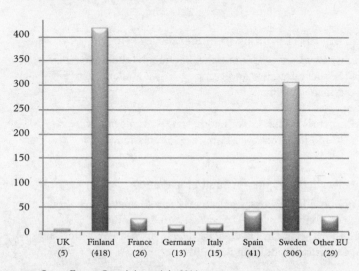

Source: Forestry Commission statistics 2014

Bibliography & Sources

Sources and further reading specific to individual species are listed with the species profiles.

General bibliography

Beckett, K. and Beckett, G., *Planting Native Trees and Shrubs*. Jarrold, 1979.

Browne, D., *Our Trees*. CVNI, 1996.

Fife, H., *Warriors and Guardians*. Argyll, 1994.

Frazer, J.G., *The Golden Bough*, Wordsworth Editions, 1993.

Mabey, R., *Food for Free*. Collins, 1972.

Mabey, R., *Flora Britannica*. Sinclair-Stevenson, 1996.

Milner, J. E., *The Tree Book*. Collins & Brown, 1992.

Stace, C., *New Flora of the British Isles*. St Edmundsbury Press, 1991

Vedel, H. and Lange, J., *Trees and Bushes in the Wood and Hedgerow*. Methuen, 1960.

Savill, P., *The Silviculture of Trees used in British Forestry*. CAB International, 1992.

All aspects of growing trees and shrubs

The new Forestry Commission handbook (although expensive) is the most practical and comprehensive guide to native woodland management:

Harmer, R., Kerr, G., & Thompson, R, *Managing Native Broadleaved Woodland*. Forestry Commission, 2010.

Seed collecting, storage, and propagating

Aldhouse J.R., *Nursery practice, Forestry Commission Bulletin 111*, 1994.

Gordon, A.G., *Seed manual for commercial forest trees*, Forestry Commission Bulletin 83, 1992.

Kiser, B., *Trees and Aftercare: A Practical Handbook*, BTCV Handbook, 1996.

Davies G., Turner, B. & Bond, B., *Weed Management for Organic farmers, Growers and Smallholders – A Complete Guide*. Crowood Press, 2008.

History of trees and woodland

Mabey, R., *Flora Britannica*, Sinclair-Stevenson, 1996.

Milliken, W., & Bridgewater, S., *Flora Celtica*, Birlinn, 2004.

Rackham, O., *History of the Countryside*.

Rackham, O., *Trees and Woodland in the British Landscape*, Weidenfeld & Nicholson, 1993.

Rackham, O., *Woodlands*, Collins, 2010

Species native to Scotland

The species profiles on the *Trees for Life* website are hard to beat:

www.treesforlife.org.uk/tfl.contents22.html

Lore

Fife, H., *Warriors & Guardians*, Argyll, 1994.

Frazer, J.G., *The Golden Bough*, Wordsworth Editions, 1993.

GLOSSARY

calyx – the outer covering of a flower or bud

cambium – the layer of growing tissue under the bark of roots and stems

carr – a dense, swampy wood of lowish stature, typically of willow and alder

coppice – trees cut back to stumps from which new growth springs

direct seeding - sowing where the tree is to grow

dioecious – having male and female flowers on different trees

drupe – a fruit with juicy flesh and a single stone, like a sloe

epiphyte – a plant growing on another plant without being parasitic

fastigiate, fastigiated – cone-shapeda fleshy cone; chiefly relates to those borne by junipers and cypresses and often mistakenly called berries.

glabrous – free from hair or down; smooth.

hybrid – the offspring of two different species

lenticel – a breathing pore in bark

mast – the seed of trees such as beech and oak, which is not set every year, but only in 'mast years'

medullary rays – bands of cells cutting radially through wood, visible in a cross section as a ray

monoecious – having both male and female flowers on the same tree

mycorrhiza – a net of fungal fibres penetrating the roots of a tree (or other plant) and supplying it with nutrients from the soil

nodulation – growth of nitrogen-fixing nodules on roots of trees such as alder which form when the correct mycorrhiza are present

origin (of seed) – a term referring to the genetic composition of the trees from which the seed is collected (see **provenance**)

ovule – unfertilised seed

pedicel – flower stalk

pinnate – having rows of leaflets on either side of a central stalk (rachis)

pollarding – the cutting of the whole crown of a tree to encourage new growth above the browse-line for animals

provenance (of seed) – a term referring to the site of the parent tree

pubescent – hairy

serotinous – late in development (or flowering)

shakes – splits that run through wood

stratify – to store seed by mixing with soil and/or sand and keeping it moist over the winter

taxa – biological categories such as species and varieties

tyloses – blockages formed in the **xylem** vessels

xylem – cells, vessels and fibres that together form the woody growing parts of the **cambium** in a tree

Index

REFORESTING SCOTLAND
Restoring the land and the people

Reforesting Scotland is a membership organisation encouraging free and open debate on a wide range of forest and land issues.

Over the years we have produced a range of projects, publications and policy statements, but what we do, individually and collectively, also goes beyond formal projects and covers a wide range of themes, many of which can be found on the organisation's website. Our activities are inspired by the Reforesting Scotland vision.

The annual Reforesting Scotland Gathering provides the opportunity for members to meet and share ideas and experiences in an informal and sociable atmosphere. Members also have an e-group through which to communicate throughout the year.

Through its international networking, Reforesting Scotland links with people-focused projects throughout the world, particularly among the temperate and boreal forest zones.

As a grassroots charity we are looking for new members who can help us take up the challenges that face Scotland's native forests and woodland culture in the future. Whatever your interest, be it as a tree grower, a craft worker, a designer of buildings, or simply as a supporter of Reforesting Scotland's aims, join Reforesting Scotland and help practical work towards the regeneration of Scotland's land and communities.

www.reforestingscotland.org

Reforesting Scotland
The Stables, Falkland Estate, Fife, KY15 7AF
info@reforestingscotland.org • 01337 857488
Registered charity number SC018032

Acknowledgements

The editor and the Directors of Reforesting Scotland would like to thank the publisher, Sara Hunt of Saraband, for her enormous contribution of time and effort in preparing this book and for co-editing this updated edition. Her support for Reforesting Scotland's desire to get the information to a wider public than the membership alone resulted in her offering two versions of the original edition of this book, although only their covers were different. Originally published in 2011 as *A Handbook of Scotland's Trees* or *The Tree Planter's Guide to the Galaxy*, the latter title harks back to the early days of the organisation. It was a nostalgic edition for members.

We would also like to thank all of the contributors who have interrupted their busy lives to write new sections, or to revise the early chapters of the book. Some of the original authors of the Profiles of Species were surprised to find an article they had written several years ago appear in their inbox or on their doormat, but all found time for rereading and revising their pieces. We are most grateful. We would also like to apologise to one, Jacqui Yelland (Hawthorn), for our failure to contact her. Many more thanks go to Michael Matthews of the Carrifran Wildwood Seed Collection Group for answering questions and supplying new information on many aspects of this book; to Professor Stephen Woodward and Stuart Fraser for their new information on invasive alien pests and pathogens, and to Anna Alexander for her patience in furnishing information whenever it was needed.

As we were preparing the final copy of the original edition we learnt that Fr. Tony Primavesi, the expert on wild roses, had died at the age of 94. Approving the republication of his *Tree Planter's Guide* article was the last piece of academic business that he carried out.

Illustration Credits

All images appearing in the black-and-white pages of this book are © 2010 Jupiter images, except for the cover and page 2 (© Carry Akroyd); pages 3, 30, 116, 159, 160, 182, 187, 192, and 198 (courtesy of Reforesting Scotland); and pages 59, 81, 151 and 181 (© Deborah White).

The photographs in the colour section appear by courtesy of Reforesting Scotland members, apart from the following: Alder, image by Nikanos; Bird cherry, image by Rasbak; Field maple, image by Rosenzweig; Hazel, image by Willow; Lodgepole pine, image by Ian Shiell (all creative commons). Tree diseases images courtesy of Prof Stephen Woollard, apart from those indicated courtesy of Kiril Sotirovski, FYR Macedonia; and Hugh Claydon, Forestry Commission Scotland.

The graphs appearing in the appendices have been prepared using statistics released by the Forestry Commission. Further information can be found on these at forestry.gov.uk.

ALSO AVAILABLE

A Handbook of Scotland's Wild Harvests
IN ASSOCIATION WITH REFORESTING SCOTLAND AND
the Scottish Wild Harvests Association

Fi Martynoga, editor

Are you a forager? If you dream of being more connected to the landscape and all the bounty it can provide, this invaluable guide will inform you about plants from fields, woods and seashores, as well as firewood and seaweeds. You'll discover well-tried recipes from Scottish kitchens and a wealth of woodland and hedgerow materials you can use in the garden or home. The individual entries abound in useful information on habitat, history, uses, lore, and how to distinguish a useful plant from similar species that are not.

A Handbook of Scotland's Coasts

Fi Martynoga, editor

This handbook is an inspirational resource for those who want to discover more about the thousands of miles of Scotland's spectacular coastlines – from its stunning geology and diverse plant, marine and bird life to its many beautiful islands, coastal history, culture and natural and built landmarks. It includes sections on coastal history and foraging as well as on great days out, whether your preference is for rockpooling, wild swimming, wildlife-watching, visiting clifftop castles or exploring historic fishing ports.

www.saraband.net